WINNING THE LOSER'S GAME

WINNING THE LOSER'S GAME

Timeless Strategies for Successful Investing

Charles D. Ellis

Third Edition

McGraw-Hill

New York   San Francisco   Washington, D.C.   Auckland   Bogotá
Caracas   Lisbon   London   Madrid   Mexico City   Milan
Montreal   New Delhi   San Juan   Singapore
Sydney   Tokyo   Toronto

Library of Congress Cataloging-in-Publication Data

Ellis, Charles D.
Winning the loser's game / Charles Ellis.
New York : McGraw-Hill, 1998.
p.   cm.
HG4529.5 .E45 1998
362.6 21
0070220107
Rev. ed of: Investment policy. 2nd ed. c1993.
Includes index.
Portfolio management.
Investment analysis.
Ellis, Charles D. Investment policy.
97053272

McGraw-Hill

A Division of The McGraw·Hill Companies

1 2 3 4 5 6 7 8 9 0 DOC/DOC 9 0 2 1 0 9 8 7

ISBN 0-07-022010-7

*The sponsoring editors for this book were Jeffrey Krames and Stephen Isaacs and
the production supervisor was Suzanne W. B. Rapcavage. It was set in Times New
Roman by North Market Street Graphics.*

Printed and bound by R. R. Donnelley & Sons Company.

The previous edition of this book was published under the title *Investment Policy*, by
Irwin Professional Publishing.

This publication is designed to provide accurate and authoritative information in
regard to the subject matter covered. It is sold with the understanding the neither the
author nor the publisher is engaged in rendering legal, accounting, or other professional service. If legal advice or other expert assistance is required, ther services of
a competent professional person should be sought.

> —*From a Declaration of Principles jointly adopted by a Committee of
> the American Bar Association and a Committee of Publishers.*

Contents

Foreword

THE FIRST TIME I encountered Charles D. Ellis (I didn't *meet* him for five more years) was in the summer of 1975, when I read his seminal article, "The Loser's Game" in *The Financial Analysts Journal.* I had already encountered future Nobel Laureate Paul Samuelson through his classic article "Challenge to Judgment" in *The Journal of Portfolio Management* a year earlier.

Together, these two articles from the intellectual world, along with some philosophical thoughts about mutual funds that I had expressed in my senior thesis at Princeton University in 1951, gave me more than enough confidence to decide, when the newly formed Vanguard Group began operations in 1975, that our very first business initiative should be the formation of the first index mutual fund in history.

To say that I remain to this day in the debt of these two brilliant men would be a rather severe understatement. Their wise contributions as investors-academics-innovators-strategists have made a difference, not only to me and to the company I founded, but to intelligent investors in all walks of life. And, as the old saw goes, "that's important, too."

Over the two-plus decades since I read those articles, index funds—owning the stock market or its subset, the Standard & Poor's 500 Stock Index—have emerged from oblivion to become a vital instrument in the investment programs of millions of investors. Today, individuals have direct investments of $200 billion in index mutual funds, and upward of $700 billion is invested for their benefit in indexed accounts by large institutional investors, pension funds, endowment funds, and the like.

I am especially delighted to write this foreword to the latest work of Charley Ellis. By doing so, I can make at least an installment payment on my debt to him, to say nothing of the debt that individual investors—directly and indirectly—owe in part to his important early insights.

But *The Loser's Game* is by no means his only contribution to the world of investing. He has also been a prolific compiler of the profound investment wisdom of the ages. *Classics* and *Classics II* should be on every serious investor's bookshelf. Most recently, *The Investor's Anthology,* published in 1997, has also become an essential reference in my own library. It is a wonderful collection of articles by philosophers and investment professionals alike, spanning the alphabet from A to Z—from Hans Christian Andersen and Warren Buffett to John Templeton and Arthur Zeikel.

His contribution to the field of investing goes well beyond the great ideas he has made so accessible to investors. Charley Ellis is above all a thoughtful developer of investment strategy, and his *Investment Policy—How to Win the Loser's Game,* first published in 1985, remains a sensible and straightforward handbook, originally designed for directors of corporations and trustees of endowment funds and later expanded to help individual investors.

In this latest incarnation of *Investment Policy,* the author has further expanded his focus to help investors in tax-deferred retirement plans, notably the 401(k) employee savings plan. These programs have fundamentally—and, I would suggest, permanently—altered the way that American families allocate their savings as they plan for their retirement years.

Today, however, many investors are making significant errors in investing for their retirement. One error is in complicating the process—owning too many mutual funds, often with only vague strategic objectives. A second is being too conservative when investing over a long time horizon—placing too much in cash reserves that provide steady but modest returns. Still a third is being too heavily dependent on owning company stock—a risk that *may* pay off, but may also result in a financial disaster. And a fourth is giving insufficient attention to plan fees and fund expenses alike, without realizing that, in the long run, *cost matters.*

Simple mathematics shows how costly these errors can be. A typical 401(k) account currently looks something like this: stocks 55 percent (one-half in company stock), and bonds 10 percent, cash reserves 35 percent. Here's what the outcome of investing $1000 per year might look like:

- If we earn an assumed 9 percent long-term annual return on a diversified portfolio of stocks *(future returns of any single common stock are utterly unpredictable)* rather than a 5 percent return on cash reserves, the return you create in stocks over an intermediate-term period (10 to 25 years) can be more than doubled in equities; over a working lifetime, the return can be nearly quadrupled.

- If we assume that investment costs at today's excessively high norms reduce those returns to 4.5 percent for cash and 7.5 percent for stocks, the added dollars you accumulate can be reduced by 10 percent or more for cash reserves and 30 percent for equities—engendering truly prodigious sacrifices in future retirement income.

These figures do not necessarily mean that investors should bet the farm on equities. They should merely realize the likely long-term cost of excessive conservatism and excessive investment expenses, and adjust their sights accordingly. For example, based on the above return and cost assumptions, an investor putting $300 per month in a retirement plan would invest $90,000 over 25 years. At the end of the period, a *market* portfolio, conservatively balanced at 30/70 in reserves and stocks, would produce a retirement fund of $283,000, while a *high-cost* portfolio, cautiously invested at 70/30 in reserves and stocks, would produce a fund of $190,000, a reduction of nearly $100,000.

Were it not ignored by so many investors, consultants, and corporations, this clear message about the value of being both a bit more venturesome and intelligently sensitive about the importance of keeping costs at minimal levels ("the cost of excessive cost") would seem obvious.

I might also emphasize that I share the author's views about the considerable importance of two other messages highlighted in this worthy book. One is the need—to the maximum extent possible—to keep emotion out of your investment program. In the business of investing, emotion inevitably leads in exactly the wrong direction—to buy stocks when you are most enthusiastic (often at market peaks) and to sell stocks when you are most worried (nearly always at market lows). If impulse is the enemy of sound long-term investing, then reason is its closest friend.

The other message is the enormous value of simplicity in investing. Counterintuitive as it may seem, complex approaches—owning too many mutual funds, expecting miracles from fund managements, trading from one speculative fund to another, engaging in market timing—are all simply counterproductive. Far better to set a sensible allocation of your assets, own a few middle-of-the-road stock funds (or one index fund), and stay the course. Simplicity is the master key to financial success.

In this new edition, Charley Ellis gives thoughtful attention to these and other issues that cry out for consideration. He shares my belief that simple approaches, combined with a few critical principles that have been affirmed by financial history, will make the difference between a perilous retirement and a comfortable one. This book will help you come to the right decisions.

John C. Bogle
Valley Forge, Pennsylvania
February 10, 1998

Preface

YOU ARE HOLDING the third edition of this book, which is embarking on its second life. The first two editions, which appeared in 1985 and 1993, were written for an audience of professional investment managers and their large clients, such as pension funds and endowments. But this institutional edition is written for a second, entirely new audience: individual investors.

The generous reception given to the previous editions—not just among directors of large corporations and trustees of prestigious endowment funds, but also among individual investors—has encouraged two decisions. One is to update the data and the dates, and the other is to address directly the quite important ways in which individual investors should think through the vital issues affecting their private investment policies, particularly those two grim factors, mortality and inflation. The focus on the needs of individual investors has been and will continue to be increasingly important as more and more people become dependent on self-directed 401(k) plans for financial security during retirement—plans that the individual participant self-directs. Freedom, particularly financial freedom, can be a two-edged sword.

This book has a long history. Increasingly aware of the great difficulty my intelligent, conscientious, and very hardworking friends were having in their quest to beat the market, in 1975 I organized my thoughts on their problem in an article entitled "The Loser's Game," which was well received within the investment profession—which is so remarkably open to ideas, particularly ideas that challenge. (It won the profession's highest award.)

While many found that provocative article a challenge to our profession, I felt challenged in a very different way. Raised in the tradition that says "If you find a problem, find a solution," I felt intrigued by the task of finding a solution to the problem identified in "The Loser's Game." As is so often true, the solution was to "think outside the box" and to *redefine* the problem. So my focus shifted from the "loser's game" (working ever harder in a futile effort to beat the market) to a "winner's game," or concentrating on the big picture of longer-term asset mix and investment policy. And so this book took shape as *Investment Policy,* a text for clients of institutional investment managers, particularly trustees of pension funds and endowments, that first appeared in 1985 and was revised and updated in 1993.

The boom in investing by individuals—particularly those who have entrusted their retirement assets to 401(k) plans and so must establish their own asset mix or investment policy—has given this book a crucial new audience: the millions of individual investors who need to know how to make their money grow successfully over the long run.

Individual investors are important to me for three major reasons: First, there are so very many of them, nearly 50 million in America and almost as many in other nations; second, almost all individual investors are truly "on their own" in designing long-term investment policies and strategies because there are few investment consultants who can afford to provide the counseling individuals need at a reasonable fee; and third, virtually all "how-to" books on investing are sold on the false promise that the typical individual can beat the professional investors. They can't and they won't.

And they don't have to. As the reader will soon see, successful investing does not depend on beating the market. Attempting to beat the market—to do better than other investors—will distract you from the fairly simple but quite interesting and productive task of designing a long-term program of investing that *will succeed* at providing the best feasible results for you.

If you feel—as I do—that some of the advice in this book is pretty simple, please keep in mind the observation of two of my best friends, who are at the peak of their distinguished careers in medicine and medical research. They agree that the two most important discoveries in medical history are *penicillin* and *washing hands* (which stopped the spreading of infection from one mother to another by the midwives who delivered most babies before 1900). What's more, my friends counsel, there's no better advice on how to live longer than to quit smoking and buckle up when driving. The lesson: advice doesn't have to be complicated to be good.

Times change, and a note of current caution may be appropriate. When this book was first written more than a decade ago, the equity market appeared significantly underpriced. Since then, America has enjoyed a remarkable bull market—one we will not see repeated from present price levels. The basic concepts and policies still hold, but their execution is no longer a "six-inch putt." Investors should be cautious at current market prices.

A large English oak table dominating the inside left corner of the Morning Room on the ground floor of Boodles, the oldest of the social clubs established more than a century ago in or near St. James's in London, is one of the places in which parts of this book were written. Other locations include hotel rooms in—and airplanes flying between—Johannesburg, San Francisco, Chicago, Nairobi, Princeton, Maine, Bermuda, Vail, Boston, New York City, and Atlanta; and of course, at home in Greenwich.

Because my priorities have been my commitments to my family and to the clients of Greenwich Associates, completing this small book has taken a very long time. This long period of gestation has been advantageous to the final result because it has given me the time and opportunity to obtain and incorporate some of the wisdom and knowledge of thoughtful others.

Several friends have given generously of their time and experience in reading and criticizing the various stages of development through which this book has passed on its way to its present form.

Claude N. Rosenberg, Jr., saved it from the oblivion to which it might have been consigned by insisting on a client focus and joshing me out of an inclination toward the stiffness of "academic" writing. Credit for readability belongs to Claude.

Dean LeBaron encouraged me with a delightful mixture of friendly admonition and cheerful *"pourquoi non?"* that must have masked some genuine doubts.

Rosalind C. Whitehead applied her brilliant talents as a writer and as an advocate for those in need as she took up the daunting task of bringing clarity to areas of uncertain explanation and took encouraging delight in the clarification.

William G. Burns, Karl Van Horn, and Chris Argyris all gave me particularly useful comments and raised questions that led to additions in several key sections that I will always want to claim.

Robert H. Jeffrey gave the kindest compliment by reading each section with the rigor of a Jesuit instructor and offered extensive suggestions on the main theory and on the structure of the argument—and even on choice of words. Tad chastised me a dozen years later—fortunately in time to influence this new edition—for giving too little attention to managing the expense of taxes. Any writer would be grateful for the chance to experience such insistent and gracious thinking and editing.

Dero Saunders applied his considerable talents as an editor and instructor in two complete rewritings. I now know why he expects to be remembered as the editor who could remove four lines from the Lord's Prayer without anyone noticing.

Paul Bourdeau of Cummings & Lockwood contributed skillfully to the concepts of estate planning.

Jason Zweig, *Money*'s wonderfully astute and insightful tribune for individual investors, gave generously of his expertise as an observer and skills as a writer and his care in improving the clarity and usefulness of every chapter. All of us are fortunate he is among us.

Susan Ellis, as she had done before, used her clarity of mind to bring order and consistency to the language and strength to the exposition.

Kimberly Breed, Lucy Carino, Ann Del Grande, Jeanne Gans, Sandy Jones, and Debra Jo Pennell, all members of Greenwich Associates, typed and retyped the all too numerous drafts through which the final text evolved.

Masanori Owa of Japan's Long-Term Credit Bank gave the sincerest and most moving compliment when he not only translated the words of this book into the Japanese language, but also translated the concepts from my culture to his—and began what has become, through a series of meetings over the years, a most happy friendship.

Special thanks are due to dozens of senior investment professionals who have participated in a series of three-day seminars on investment policy and practice—sponsored by my friends and former partners at Donaldson, Lufkin, and Jenrette—which it has been my great privilege to lead for nearly 30 years. Many of the ideas in the book have been developed at these seminars. Others were developed with and for the graduate students I so enjoyed teaching at Harvard Business School and the Yale School of Management and the participants at AIMR's in-service course for senior professionals given each summer at Princeton.

Finally, I wish to recognize explicitly my admiration and respect for the large number of extraordinarily talented, resourceful, and hardworking men and women who compete for success at our nation's investing institutions and securities firms. It is a profound but ironic compliment that their skillful striving is what has made it possible to propose the approach to investment policy advocated in this book.

Charles D. Ellis

Introduction

DO INVESTORS
MATTER?

YOU WILL NOT LEARN HOW to *invest* by reading this book, but you can learn in less than 150 pages how to be a successful *investor*—and to know you have designed a program of investing that will, almost inevitably, provide the results that are best for you and your purposes and are feasible within the realistic limits of the capital markets.

In this sense, after you read this book, you will know and understand all you will ever need to know and understand to be a truly successful investor. For such a small book, this ambition may seem far too bold. But there is a countervailing modesty.

This book does not intend to explain how to be successful at traditional investment management—how to pick stocks, time markets, or execute major strategic shifts in a portfolio. Such a treatise would certainly require far greater length. It would be written for professional investment managers as producers and sellers of investment services. And it would be based on the assumption that it is feasible to outperform other investors in the active-aggressive kind of investment management that dominates institutional investing today. This basic assumption must now be seriously questioned*— precisely because so many talented, informed, experienced, and diligent professionals are working so hard at institutional investing that they make it unrealistic for any one manager to outperform these other professionals.

This book is different. Far from accepting the conventional wisdom that talented, competitive, professional investment managers can beat the market, it questions closely the whole concept of institutional investing as it is practiced today.

This book is not written for the sellers of investment management services. It is written for the buyers who, as clients of professional investment managers, have a real responsibility to themselves to understand the basic nature of institutional investing, why investment managers succeed or fail, and what can be done to achieve long-term investment success, even when most professional investment managers are failing to beat the market to achieve long-term investment success.

This consumers' guide to investment management is designed to meet the needs of the many individual investors who entrust their family savings to mutual funds, trust companies, and investment advisors; the needs of the corporate executives and union and public officials responsible for pension funds; and the needs of the men and women who serve as trustees of the endowments of universities, museums, schools, hospitals, and foundations.

This book is written with a clear point of view: investors all too often delegate—or more accurately abdicate—to their investment managers responsibilities which they can and should keep for themselves. Their undelegatable responsibilities are: setting explicit investment policies consistent with their objectives, defining long-range objectives appropriate to their particular fund, and managing their managers to ensure that their policies are being followed.

This book is a guide for those who will accept this central client responsibility and who want to be successful at achieving their true and realistic objectives.

Much as it might seem obvious that client investors should care a lot about the way their money is managed, the reality is they typically do almost nothing about it—until it's too late. In short, this book is written for investors who are prepared to take charge of their own investment destiny.

---

*Thirty years ago when I was writing *Institutional Investing* (published by BUSINESS ONE IRWIN) it made sense to prescribe and advocate a strategic approach to active management. Today, the world of investment management is different, and the time has come for a different concept of the problem of investing and an appropriately different concept of the solution.

Despite the fact that everybody "knows" that each family's funds—and each pension fund or endowment fund—differs in situation from every other fund (and that these differences are often quite substantial), and despite the conventional consensus that these substantial differences should be reflected in different investment policies and practices, the plain fact is that the investment portfolios of most funds are very much alike.

This is not the way it should be. The needs and purposes of investors—whether individuals or corporations or universities—are not the same, and their investment portfolios should not be the same. And the relationships between managers and clients are not and should not be the same. Some clients are sophisticated experts, others are not. As the clients' knowledge differs, so their relationship with managers should differ.

Without clear direction from their investor clients, it is natural for investment managers to move toward the center, to put portfolios in neutral, to be conventional. (It is also easier to treat all investors the same.) In other words, investment managers will tend to produce average portfolios for *all* their clients rather than portfolios that are carefully designed to meet the particular objectives of each individual investor.

At the same time, ironically, professional investment managers lament over and over again that they feel they must compromise their investment decisions because clients do not do their part. In particular, managers believe they could achieve far better results if their clients took a longer-term view of the investment process and if their clients would only be more specific about the kind of investment portfolio they really want.

Clients "own" the central responsibility for formulating and assuring implementation of long-term investment policy. This responsibility cannot be delegated to investment managers; it is *your* job, not theirs. Fortunately, this client responsibility can be fulfilled without extensive experience in the operational complexities of contemporary securities analysis or portfolio management.

To fulfill your responsibilities to yourself, you need three characteristics: (1) a genuine interest in developing an understanding of your own true interests and objectives, (2) an appreciation of the fundamental nature of capital markets and investments, and (3) the discipline to work out the basic policies that will, over time, succeed in fulfilling your realistic investment objectives. Individual investors—other than the very wealthy—will not be in a good position to negotiate or even discuss their investment needs and how professional investment managers can or should meet those needs. But even the smallest individual investor can take the time to find a good match between what is truly in his or her individual best interest with the investment services (most likely mutual funds) offered by capable and committed investment organizations. That's what this book is about.

Professional investment managers will also find this book useful in providing a context for the work to which they devote so much of their time and skill—the day-to-day management of investment portfolios. Managers should encourage their clients to use this book as a guide to performing the vital role of being informed, active, and therefore *successful* clients.

While it is a spirited critique of contemporary investment practice, this book is by no means a condemnation of investment managers. The problem is not that professional managers lack skill or diligence. Quite the opposite. The problem with trying to beat the market is that professional investors are so talented, so numerous, and so dedicated to their work that as a group they make it very difficult for any one of their number to do significantly better than the others, particularly in the long run.

There are two different kinds of problems in trying to beat the market. One problem is that it is so extraordinarily difficult to do—and so easy, while trying to do better, to do *worse.* The other problem with targeting on "beating the market" as your primary investment objective is that you will thereby divert both your own attention and that of your investment manager from the need to establish long-range objectives and investment policies that are well matched to your particular needs. (Individual investors with a pressing short-term need—whether immediate or within the next five years—should separate the funds required to meet this need so the rest of their investments can be managed for the longer term.)

The real purpose of investment management is not to "beat the market," but to do what is really right for a particular client. And making sure the manager concentrates on achieving that objective is, by default, the responsibility of the client.

Do investors matter? Indeed they *should.* But you will only matter if you assert your authority and fulfill these responsibilities: deciding investment objectives, developing sound investment policies, and holding your portfolio managers accountable for implementing long-term investment policy in the daily portfolio operations.

1

THE LOSER'S GAME

DISAGREEABLE DATA ARE STEADILY STREAMING out of the computers of the performance measurement firms. Over and over again, these facts and figures inform us that investment managers are failing to "perform," that is, to beat the market. Occasional periods of above-average results raise expectations that are soon dashed as false hopes. Contrary to their often articulated goal of outperforming the market averages, the nation's professional investment managers are not beating the market; the market is beating them.

Faced with information that contradicts what they believe, humans tend to respond in one of two ways. Some will ignore the new knowledge and hold to their former beliefs. Others will accept the validity of the new information, factor it into their perception of reality, and then put it to use.

Investment management, as traditionally practiced, is based on a single basic belief: Professional investment managers *can* beat the market. That premise appears to be false (see Figure 1-1).

If the premise that it is feasible to outperform the market were true, then deciding *how* to go about achieving success would be a matter of straightforward logic.

First, since the overall market can be represented by a passive and public listing such as the Standard & Poor's 500 Stock Index, the successful manager need only rearrange his portfolios more productively than the

1

FIGURE 1-1   Equity mutual funds outperformed by S&P 500 index

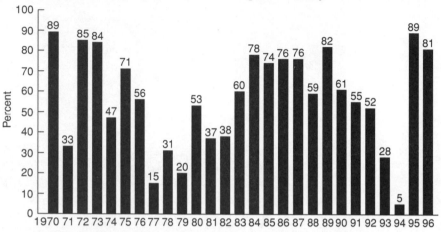

"mindless" S&P 500. He can be different in stock selection, or strategic emphasis on particular groups of stocks, or market timing, or in various combinations of these.

Second, since the active manager will want to make as many "right" decisions as possible, he will assemble a group of bright, well-educated, highly motivated, hardworking professionals whose collective purpose will be to identify underpriced securities to buy and overpriced securities to sell—and to beat the market by shrewdly betting against the crowd.

Investment managers are not beating the market; the market is beating them.

Unhappily, the basic assumption that most institutional investors can outperform the market is false. The institutions *are* the market. They cannot, as a group, outperform themselves. In fact, given the cost of active management—fees, commissions, and so forth—most investment managers will, over the long term, underperform the overall market.

Because investing institutions are so numerous and capable and determined to do well for their clients, investment management is not a "winner's game." It has become a loser's game.

Before analyzing what happened to convert institutional investing from a winner's game to a loser's game, consider the profound difference between these two kinds of games. In a winner's game, the outcome is determined by the correct actions of the *winner.* In a loser's game, the outcome is determined by mistakes made by the *loser.*

Dr. Simon Ramo, an eminent scientist at TRW Inc., identified the crucial difference between a winner's game and a loser's game in his excellent book on playing strategy, *Extraordinary Tennis for the Ordinary Tennis Player.*[1] Over many years, Dr. Ramo observed that tennis was not one game, but two—one played by professionals and a very few gifted amateurs; the other played by all the rest of us.

Investing has changed from a winner's game to a loser's game.

Although players in both games use the same equipment, dress, rules, and scoring, and conform to the same etiquette and customs, they play two very different games. After extensive scientific and statistical analysis, Dr. Ramo summed it up this way: Professionals *win* points; amateurs *lose* points.

In expert tennis, the ultimate outcome is determined by the actions of the winner. Professional tennis players stroke the ball hard, with laserlike precision, through long and often exciting rallies, until one player is able to drive the ball just out of reach or force the other player to make an error. These splendid players seldom make mistakes.

Amateur tennis, Dr. Ramo found, is almost entirely different. Brilliant shots, long and exciting rallies, and seemingly miraculous recoveries are few and far between. Instead, the ball is often hit into the net or out of bounds, and double faults at service are not uncommon. The amateur seldom beats his *opponent,* but he beats *himself* all the time. The victor in this game of tennis gets a higher score *because his opponent is losing even more points.*

As a scientist and statistician, Dr. Ramo gathered data to test his hypothesis in a clever way. Instead of keeping conventional game scores— love, 15 all, 30–15, and so forth—Ramo simply counted points won versus points lost. He found that in expert tennis about 80 percent of the points are won, but in amateur tennis about 80 percent of the points are lost.

The two games are fundamental opposites. Professional tennis is a winner's game: the outcome is determined by the actions of the winner. Ama-

[1]Simon Ramo, *Extraordinary Tennis for the Ordinary Tennis Player* (New York: Crown Publishers, 1977).

teur tennis is a loser's game: the outcome is determined by the actions of the loser—who defeats himself.

Distinguished military historian Admiral Samuel Elliot Morison makes a similar central point in his thoughtful treatise *Strategy and Compromise:* "In warfare, mistakes are inevitable. Military decisions are based on estimates of the enemy's strengths and intentions that are usually faulty, and on intelligence that is never complete and often misleading. Other things being equal," concludes Morison, "the side that makes the fewest strategic errors wins the war."[2]

War is the ultimate loser's game. Golf is another. Tommy Armour, in his great book *How to Play Your Best Golf All the Time,* says: "The best way to win is by making fewer bad shots,"[3] an observation with which all weekend golfers would concur. There are many other loser's games. Some, like institutional investing, were once winner's games, but have changed into loser's games with the passage of time. For example, 70 or 80 years ago only very brave, athletic, strong-willed young people with good eyesight had the nerve to try flying an airplane. In those glorious days, flying was a winner's game. But times have changed and so has flying. If the pilot of your 747 came aboard today wearing a 50-mission hat with a long, white silk scarf around his neck, you'd get off. Such people no longer belong in airplanes because flying today is a loser's game with one simple rule: Don't make mistakes.

Likewise, the "money game" we call investment management has evolved in recent decades from a winner's game to a loser's game.[4] A basic change has occurred in the investment environment; the market came to be dominated in the 1970s by the very institutions that were striving to win by outperforming the market. In just 10 years, the market activities of the investing institutions shifted from only 30 percent of total public transactions to an overwhelming 80 percent. And that shift made all the difference. No longer was the active investment manager competing with cautious custodians or amateurs who were out of touch with the market: Now he was competing with other experts.

The money game includes a formidable group of competitors. At least 200 major institutional investors and another 1,000 small- and medium-sized institutions operate in the market all day, every day, in the most

---

[2]Samuel Elliot Morison, *Strategy and Compromise* (New York: Little Brown, 1958).

[3]Tommy Armour, *How to Play Your Best Golf All the Time* (New York: Simon & Schuster, 1971).

[4]Perhaps winners' games self-destruct because they attract too many players—all of whom want to win. (That's why gold rushes finish ugly.)

intensely competitive way. The 50 largest, most active institutions do 50 percent of all the trades in the market. So about half the time we buy and about half the time we sell, the "other fellow" is one of these giant professionals, with all their resources.

The key question under the new rules of the game is this: How much better must the active manager be to *at least* recover the costs of active management? The answer is daunting. If we assume 80 percent portfolio turnover (implying that the fund manager holds typical stock for 15 months, which is approximately average for the fund industry) and total trading costs (commission plus the "spread") of 1 percent to buy and 1 percent to sell (again, average rates), plus a fee for active management of 1.25 percent (slightly below average among U.S. stock mutual funds), then the typical fund's operating costs are 2.85 percent per year.[5]

Recovering these costs is surprisingly difficult. For example, assuming an average annual rate of return of 10 percent for stocks, then the active manager must overcome the drag of 2.85 percent annual operating costs. If the fund manager is only to match the market's 10 percent return after all costs, then he or she must return 12.85 percent before his costs. In other words, for you merely to do as well as the market, your fund manager must be able to outperform it by 28.5 percent![6]

The stark reality is that most money managers have been losing the money game. The historical record is that in the 25 years ending with 1997, on a cumulative basis, over three-quarters of professionally managed funds underperformed the S&P 500 Market Stock Average.

Thus, the burden of proof is on the person who says, "I am a winner, I can win the money game." Because only a sucker backs a false "winner" in a loser's game, investors have a right to demand that the investment manager explain exactly what he or she is going to do and why it is going to work so very well.

---

[5](0.4 percent + .60 × [1 percent + 1 percent]). Far more than brokerage commissions and dealer spreads are properly included in transactions costs. The best way to show how large transactions costs really are is to compare the *theoretical* results of a "paper portfolio" with the *actual* results of a "real money portfolio." Experts will tell you the differences are always impressive. And there's yet another cost of transactions—the cost of unwisely getting into stocks you would not have attempted if you were not "sure" you could get out at any time because the market looks so liquid. This is a real liquidity trap. Think how differently people would behave on the highway or in the bedroom if they were not so sure they'd not be caught. It's the same way in investments: you don't always get caught nor do you always *not* get caught. *All* of these costs are part of the *total transactions costs.*

[6]Which makes the sustained superior performance of Warren Buffet and John Neff so very wonderful.

If investment managers are on balance not beating the market, then investors certainly should at least consider joining it by investing in passive index funds that replicate the market. The data from the performance measurement firms suggest that an index fund would have outperformed most investment managers over long periods of time.

The reason that investing has become a loser's game, especially for the professionals who manage the leading mutual funds and investment management organizations, is that in the complex problem each manager is trying to solve, his efforts, and the efforts of his many determined competitors, to find a solution have become the dominant variables. And their efforts to beat the market are no longer the most important part of the solution; they are the most important part of the problem.

For any one manager to outperform the other professionals, he must be so skillful and so quick that he can regularly catch other professionals making errors—and can systematically exploit those errors faster than other professionals can. It was one thing a generation ago when the aggressive professionals were few and did less than 10 percent of the buying and selling. In those easy, gentle days of 1960, 90 percent of the activity on the New York Stock Exchange was buying and selling by *individuals*. The professionals were in a happy minority. They had lots of "targets of opportunity." No more. Now, it's just the other way around: 90 percent of the trading is by seasoned *professionals*. Sure, they each make errors and mistakes, but the other pros are always looking for any error and will pounce on it just as quickly as they can. Attractive investment opportunities simply don't come often, and the few that do don't last very long. Yes, some professionals do beat the market in any particular year or in any decade, but scrutiny of the records reveals that very few professionals beat the market averages over the long haul. And even more discouraging to investors searching for superior managers, those managers that have had superior results in the past are unlikely to have superior results in the *future*. In investment performance, the past is *not* prologue. Regression to the mean (the tendency for behavior to move toward "normal" or average) is a persistently powerful phenomenon in physics and sociology—and in investing. So many professional investment managers are so good, they make it nearly impossible for any one professional to outperform the market they together now dominate.

The beginning of wisdom for you is to understand that few—if any— major investment organizations will outperform the market averages over long periods of time and that it is very difficult to estimate which managers will outperform.

The next step is to decide whether—even if it could be won—this loser's game would be worth playing.

2

BEATING THE MARKET

THE ONLY WAY TO BEAT THE MARKET, after adjusting for market risk, is to discover and exploit other investors' mistakes.

It can be done. And it has been done by most investors some of the time. But very few investors have been able to outsmart and outmaneuver other investors enough to beat the market consistently over the long term.

Active investment managers can work on any or all of four investment vectors:

1. Market timing.
2. Selection of specific stocks or groups of stocks.
3. Changes in portfolio structure or strategy.
4. An insightful, long-term investment concept or philosophy.

Even the most casual observer of markets and securities will be impressed by the simply splendid array of apparent opportunities to do better than "settle for average." The price charts for the overall market, for major industry groups, and for individual stocks make it seem deceptively "obvious" that active investors can do better. After all, we can see with our own eyes that Michael Jordan, Tiger Woods, and Cindy Crawford are, each in their own ways, consistently above average. Why, then, should some investment managers not also be consistently above average? In short, why should it be so hard to beat the market?

MARKET TIMING

The most audacious way to increase potential returns is market timing. The classic market timer moves the portfolio in and out of the market so it is, he hopes, fully invested during rising markets and out of the market when prices are falling. Another form of timing would shift an equity portfolio out of stock groups that are expected to underperform the market and into groups that may outperform it.

In a bond portfolio the market timer hopes to shift into long maturities before falling interest rates drive up long bond prices and back into short maturities before rising interest rates drive long bond prices down.

The only way to beat the market is to exploit other investors' mistakes.

In a balanced portfolio the market timer strives to invest more heavily into stocks when they will produce greater total returns than bonds, then shift into bonds when they will produce greater total returns than equities, and into short-term investments when they can produce greater total returns than either bonds or stocks.

A delightful comparative analysis of two kinds of investment perfection for the period 1940–73 gives a sense of the seductive "potential" of market timing. The first record was the result of perfect market timing with 100 percent in stocks in all rising markets and 100 percent in cash in all falling markets.

With 22 transactions (11 buys and 11 sells) in 34 years, and using the Dow Jones Industrial Average as a proxy for stocks, $1,000 was expanded into $85,937.

During the same 34-year period, with the hypothetical portfolio always 100 percent invested and always invested in the one best industry group, the same $1,000 (with 28 buys and 28 sells) exploded into $4,357,000,000! The last two years indicate the pluck requisite to the process: In January 1971, $687 million was invested in restaurant companies and became $1.7 billion by year end, and was then committed to gold stocks which carried it up to $4.4 billion by Christmas! Of course this example is absurd. It has never been done and never will be done. More important, even far less magical results have not and will not be achieved through "timing" because no one manager is so much more astute than his or her professional competitors on a repetitive basis.

Despite the enticing appeal of reducing market exposure by astute sales when securities appear to be overpriced, and boldly reinvesting when prices appear to have declined to attractive low levels—selling high and buying low—the overwhelming evidence shows that market timing is not an effective way to increase returns for one dour but compelling reason: on average and over time, *it does not work.*

The evidence on investment managers' success with market timing is impressive—and overwhelmingly negative. One careful study of market timing concluded that an investment manager would have to be right on his market forecast 75 percent of the time for his portfolio just to *break even* after measuring the costs of mistakes and the costs of transactions. Robert Jeffrey has explained why it is so difficult to improve results with market timing: so much of the "action" occurs in such brief periods and at times when investors are most likely to be captives of a conventional consensus. An unpublished study of 100 large pension funds and their experience with market timing found that while all the funds had engaged in at least some market timing, not one of the funds had improved its rate of return as a result of its efforts at timing. In fact, 89 of the 100 lost as a result of "timing"—and their losses averaged a daunting 4.5 percent over the five-year period.

Just as there are *old* pilots and there are *bold* pilots, there are no old bold pilots; and there are *no* investors who have achieved recurring successes in market timing. Decisions that are driven by either greed or fear are usually wrong, usually late, and very unlikely to be reversed correctly. Particularly with real money, don't even *consider* trying to outguess the market or outmaneuver the professionals to "sell high" and to "buy low." You'll fail, perhaps disastrously.

As Fischer Black put it, "The market does just as well, on average, when the investor is *out* of the market as it does when he is *in*. So he loses money, relative to a simple buy-and-hold strategy, by being out of the market part of the time."

Perhaps the best insight into the difficulties in market timing came from an experienced professional's candid lament: "I've seen lots of interesting approaches to market timing—and I have tried most of them in my 40 years of investing. They may have been great before my time, but not one of them worked for me. Not one!"

The case for *not* attempting market timing is partly that the history of many, many investment managers shows that the market does as well when they are heavily in cash as it does when they are fully invested—and vice versa. (In fact, professional investment managers usually cancel each other out; the number who are increasing cash in each period is typically equal to the number who are reducing cash during the same period.)

The second reason is even more striking. Figure 2-1 shows what happens to long-term compound returns when the best days are removed from the record. Taking out the 10 best days—less than ½ of 1 percent of the period examined—cuts the average rate of return by one third from 18 percent to 12 percent. Taking the 10 next best days away cuts returns almost another one third to 8.3 percent. Removing a total of 20 days—1½ percent of the total period—cuts returns from 18 percent to 5 percent. Figure 2-2 shows a similar result when the best *years* are excluded from the calculation of the long-term averages. Market timing is a "wicked" idea. Don't try it—ever. Still, if you believe, as do all great litigators, that good preparation requires mastery of your opponent's case, you may be interested in an insider's debate among investment professionals on the seductive *possibilities* of market timing. A dollar invested in the S&P 500 from January 1960 to June 1990 would have compounded to $19.45. Now watch: If the same dollar had been taken out of the market for the *best 10 months* of those three decades—for just 3 percent of the whole 30-year period—the value at the end of the period would have been only $6.58 (i.e., only about as good as the parsimonious T-bill). So, say the "long-termers," stay invested through the rough times: That's the only sane way to be there so you'll enjoy the great and good times!

Market timing is a "wicked" idea.
Don't try it—ever.

Not so fast, say the "timers." If the 10 *worst* months had been avoided, the fund would have climbed to $63.39. Should you find this if-only sort of thinking entrancing, you'll probably enjoy rereading James Thurber's classic, *The Adventures of Walter Mitty.*

Using the S&P 500 average returns, the story is told quickly and clearly: Almost all the total returns on stocks in the 70 long years from 1926 to 1996 were achieved in the best 60 months—only 7 percent of the 862 months over those long years. Imagine the profits if we could know which months! But we cannot and will not. What we do know is both simple and valuable: If we missed those few and fabulous 60 best months, we would have missed

almost all the total returns accumulated over two full generations. The lesson is clear: You have to be there "when lightening strikes."

There is no evidence of any large institutions having anything like consistent ability to get in when the market is low and get out when the market
is high. Attempts to switch between stocks and bonds, or between stock and
cash, in anticipation of market moves, have been unsuccessful much more
often than they have been successful.

STOCK SELECTION

The second tactical way to increase returns is through stock selection or
"stock picking." Professional investors devote an extraordinary amount of
skill, time, and effort to this work. Stock valuation dominates the research
efforts of investing institutions and the research services of stock brokers.

Through financial analysis or field studies of competitors and suppli-
ers as well as management interviews, investors seek to attain a better
understanding of the investment value of a security or group of securities
than the market consensus. When investment managers find significant
differences between the market price and the value of a security (as they
appraise it), they can buy or sell, as appropriate, to capture the differential
between the market's price and the true investment value for their clients'
portfolios.

Unfortunately, however, security analysis—taken as a whole—does not
appear to be a useful or profitable activity. The stocks investment managers

FIGURE 2-1   Compound returns (%) 1982 through 1990
Courtesy of Cambridge Associates.

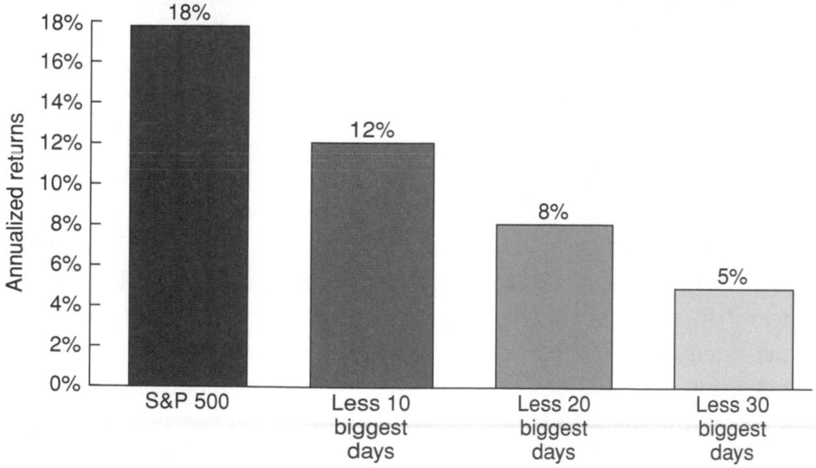

FIGURE 2-2   Cumulative returns ($) one dollar invested 1928 through 1990

Courtesy of Cambridge Associates.

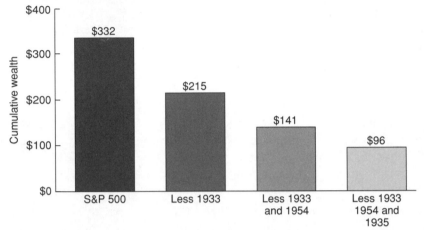

sell after doing fundamental research, and the stocks they don't buy, typically do as well as the stocks they do buy (because they sell from each other and buy from each other, making the market "efficient").

Again, the problem is not that investment research is not done well. The problem is that it is done so very well by so many—particularly by the research analysts at major brokerage firms, who share their information and evaluations almost instantly through global information networks with hundreds of professional investors who take swift reactive action, often striving to act quickly in anticipation of how others will soon act—that no one group of investors is likely to gain a regular and repetitive useful advantage over all other investors. And the only way to beat the market is to beat the other professionals who, as a group, *are* the market.

PORTFOLIO STRATEGY

Strategic decisions—in both stock and bond portfolios—involve major commitments that affect the overall structure of the portfolio. They are made to exploit insights into major industry groups or changes in the economy and interest rates or anticipated shifts in the valuation of major types of stocks such as "emerging growth" stocks or "basic industry" stocks. Each of these judgments involves what can be described as market segment risk.

For example, in 1980 portfolio managers who invested heavily in two areas—oil and technology—had very favorable results compared to investors who chose instead to invest heavily in utilities and other interest-sensitive stocks or in consumer stocks. Equally important, they had to be out of energy stocks in 1981 or they would "give it all back."

In the early 1970s, portfolio managers who invested heavily in large capitalization growth stocks—the "nifty 50"—experienced exceptionally favorable results as the notorious "two tier" market developed.[1] In the later 1970s, these same securities produced exceptionally negative results when previously anticipated earnings failed to materialize and institutions became disenchanted with the concept and dumped their holdings, which collapsed the price/earnings (P/E) ratios and brought stock prices way down. The same sort of thing later happened with small high-tech stocks, which appreciated far faster than the market from 1980 to 1983 and then fell much faster in 1984. In the late 1980s and in 1990, "value" stocks (which had outperformed the market for a decade) plunged, reversing much of the prior 10 years' gains.

As the well-worn saying goes, it is not a stock market but a market of stocks—one that lures portfolio managers (but not without peril) to make major strategic decisions on groups of stocks in the portfolios they manage.

Full of interesting potential—being in the right place at the right time—this approach to investing challenges the manager to discover the new (and often unfamiliar) way to invest as markets shift, become proficient at each new way, and then abandon it for another new way. (Of course, in theory, it can be done, but will it be done? By which managers? For how long?)

INVESTMENT PHILOSOPHY

The fourth possible way to increase returns is to develop a profound and valid insight into the forces that drive a particular sector of the market or a particular group of companies or industries and systematically exploit that investment insight or concept.

Investing to exploit an investment concept or philosophy involves an enduring investment commitment—through cycle after cycle in the stock market and in the business economy—for an individual portfolio manager or an entire investment management organization.

An organization that is committed, for example, to growth stock investing will concentrate on evaluating new technologies, understanding the management skills required to lead rapidly growing organizations, and ana-

[1]Growth stocks had a much higher P/E ratio than industrial stocks, dividing the market into two tiers.

lyzing the financial requirements of investing in new markets and new products to sustain growth. This investment organization will, it is hoped, learn from experience—no doubt sometimes painful experience—how to discriminate between ersatz "growth stocks" that fizzle out and true growth companies that will achieve success over many years.

Other investment management organizations take the view that among the many large corporations in mature and often cyclical industries, there are always some that have considerably greater investment value than is recognized by other investors; that with astute research these superior values can be isolated; and that by buying good values at depressed prices these investment managers can achieve superior returns for their clients with relatively low risk. Such organizations will develop considerable expertise in "separating the wheat from the chaff," avoiding the low-priced stocks that *ought* to be low priced, and ferreting out insights into investment value that other investors have not yet recognized.

Among the variety of different concepts of investing that can be pursued over many, many years, one emphasizes medium-sized growth companies in specialized industries while another focuses on assets rather than earnings with confidence that carefully chosen, well-positioned assets can and will some day be redeployed to earn good profits. Another group of "contrary opinion" investors will concentrate on stocks that are clearly out of favor with most investors, confident that by looking where prices are depressed, and analyzing many companies dispassionately, they will find bargains.

The important test of an investment concept or philosophy is the manager's ability to adhere to it for valid, long-term reasons—even when the short-term results are most disagreeable and disheartening. Persistence can lead to mastery and development of an important distinctive competence in the particular kind of investing in which the manager specializes.

The great advantage to the conceptual or philosophical approach is that the investment firm can organize itself to do its own particular kind of investing all the time, avoid the noise and confusion of alternatives, attract investment analysts and managers interested in and skilled at the particular type of investing, and through continuous practice, self-critique, and study to master it. The great disadvantage is that if the chosen kind of investing becomes obsolete or out of touch with the changing market, a proficient specialist organization is most unlikely to detect the need for change until it is too late.

What is remarkable about these profound investment concepts is how few have been discovered that last for very long—most likely because the hallmark of a free capital market is that few if any opportunities to establish a proprietary long-term competitive advantage can be found and maintained for a long time.

All four of these basic forms of active investing have one fundamental characteristic in common: *They depend on the errors of others.* Whether by omission or commission, the only way in which a profit opportunity can be available to the active investor—in an individual stock or a group of stocks—is that the consensus of other professional investors is *wrong.* While this collective error does occur, we must ask how often these errors are made and how often we would avoid the normal errors being made by others and have the wisdom and courage to take action opposite the consensus!

With so many competitors seeking superior insight into the value/price relationship of individual stocks or industry groups, and with so much information so widely and rapidly communicated throughout the investment community, the chances of discovering and exploiting profitable insights into individual stocks or groups of stocks—opportunities left behind by the errors and inattention of other investors—are certainly not richly promising.

With so many apparent opportunities to do better than the market, it must be disconcerting for investment managers—and their clients—to see how hard it is for investment managers, in fact, to do better than the market after adjustment for risk[2] over the long haul. Yet even the most talented investment manager must wonder how he can expect his hardworking and determined competitors to provide him—through incompetence, error, or inattention—with sufficiently attractive opportunities to buy or sell in size on significantly advantageous terms on a regular basis so he can "beat the market" by beating them. The stock market is fascinating *and* very deceptive—in the *short* run. In the very *long* run, the market is almost boringly reliable and predictable. The gremlin is Mr. Market. He's a mischievous but fascinating fellow who persistently teases investors with such gimmicks and tricks as surprising earnings, startling dividend announcements, sudden surges of inflation, inspiring presidential pronouncements, grim reports of commodity prices, announcements of amazing new technologies, ugly bankruptcies, and even threats of war. These events come from his bag of tricks when least expected. Just as magicians use clever deceptions to divert our attention, Mr. Market's very short-term distractions can trick us and confuse our thinking about investments.

[2]See Chapter 1 for an explanation.

The daily weather is comparably different from the climate. *Weather* is about the short run; *climate* is about the long run. And that makes all the difference. In choosing a *climate* in which to build a home, we would not be deflected by last week's *weather.* Similarly, in choosing a long-term investment program, we don't want to be deflected by temporary market conditions.

If you—like Walter Mitty—still fantasize that you can and will beat the pros, you'll need both luck and prayer.

Let's ignore that rascal, Mr. Market, and his constant jumping around. Let's recognize that the daily quotation of the DJIA is no more important to a long-term investor than the daily weather is to a climatologist or to a family deciding where to make their permanent home. Let's concentrate on real results over the long term.

Investors who studiously ignore the deceptive tricks of Mr. Market and pay no attention to current prices will look instead at their *real* investments in *real* companies—and to their growing earnings and dividends.

In the movie *Full Metal Jacket,* two drill sergeants are watching their basic training class jogging in close-order drill to their graduation ceremony, shouting military calls like: "Airborne! All the way!" One drill sergeant says, "Sarge, what do you see when you look at those boys?" After the classic expectoration, the other replies, "What do I see? I'll tell yeh. About 10 percent of those boys are honest to God *real* soldiers!" Pause. "The rest are just . . . targets!"

Las Vegas is busy every day—so we know not everyone is rational. If you—like Walter Mitty—still fantasize that you can and will beat the pros, you'll need both luck and prayer.

3

THE POWERFUL PLODDER

THE LARGEST PART OF ANY PORTFOLIO'S total long-term returns will come from the simplest investment decision that can be made, and by far the easiest to implement: buying the market.

Hopelessly unpopular with investment managers and with most clients, the uninspiring, dull "market portfolio" (or "index fund") is seldom given anything like the respect it deserves.

Plodding along in its unimaginative, inexpensive, "no brain" way, this "plain Jane" form of investing will, over time, achieve better results than most professional investment managers.

Active investment managers—particularly those with good records—accept the proposition that the market portfolio achieves good long-term returns, but they see an opportunity and challenge to do better. "Even 1 percent on a $100 million or $500 million portfolio is a lot of money—particularly when it's 1 percent compounded year after year—and well worth going after."

They may be right. Some *will* be right. But clients should know that they won't *all* be right. Indeed, the evidence so far is that a great majority of managers will not. Their clients would have done better in a market fund.[1]

Considering the time, cost, and effort devoted to achieving better than market results, the index fund certainly produces a lot for a little. This dull workhorse portfolio may appear virtually mindless, but is, in fact, based on an extensive body of research about markets and investments that is well worth examining and can be summarized briefly.

To summarize, the securities market is an open, free, and competitive market in which large numbers of well-informed and price-sensitive investors and professional investment managers compete skillfully, vigorously, and continuously as both buyers and sellers. Nonexperts can easily retain the services of experts. Prices are quoted widely and promptly. Effective prohibitions against market manipulations are established. And arbitrageurs, traders, market technicians, and longer-term "fundamental" investors seek to find and profit from any market imperfections. Such a market is considered "efficient."[2] In an efficient market, changes in prices will follow the pattern described as a "random walk," which means even close observers of the market—"tape readers"—will not be able to find patterns in securities prices with which to predict future price changes on which they can make profits.

Moreover, because other competing investors are well-informed buyers and sellers, particularly when they are considered in the aggregate, it will be unlikely that any one investment manager can regularly obtain profit increments for a large portfolio through fundamental research, because so many other equally dedicated professionals will also be using the best research they can obtain to make their appraisals of whether and when to sell or buy. The more you believe the market is efficient, the more you will believe the rule that the more numerous the skillful competitors, the less likely anyone will achieve consistently superior results.

In a perfectly efficient market, prices not only reflect any information that could be inferred from the historical sequence of prices, but also incor-

---

[1] One caution is important regarding "market" funds. Significant sectors are left out of the traditional market indexes. Some of the most interesting and rewarding areas of investing in the past decade—particularly small company stocks—are either not included in the index or are underrepresented. And all the international markets—more than half of the world market—are not included. To compensate for these gaps, new "extended" market funds are being designed to capture the "whole" market.

[2] Not perfect, and not even perfectly efficient, but sufficiently efficient that wise investors will not expect to be able to exploit its inefficiencies regularly.

porate and impound all that is knowable[3] about the companies whose stocks are being traded. An efficient market does not mean that stocks will always sell at the "right" price. Investors can be quite *wrong* in their judgments—overly optimistic, overly pessimistic—and this will show up in later changes in prices. A market can be quite clumsy on valuations and still be very efficient on market information and on fundamental information about companies. (That's why the best opportunities for active investment managers to add value may well come from being wiser and less susceptible to the psychology of the crowd than others.)

America's most successful investor, Warren Buffet, recommends that individual investors consider indexing.

The index fund provides investment managers and their clients with an easy alternative. They do not have to play the more complex games of equity investing unless they *want* to play.

This is a marvelous freedom of choice. The option to use the index fund enables any investment manager always to keep pace with the market virtually without effort. It allows you to play only when and where and only for so long as you really want to—and to select any part of the wide investment spectrum for deliberate action at any time for as long or as brief a period as you wish.

For investors, even those who are clients, the ability to call "time out" and to invest at any time in an index fund is an important advantage because superior knowledge and skill are not consistent attributes of investment managers. Superior knowledge is a *variable*. This freedom not to play carries the reciprocal responsibility to play only for cause, and only when the incremental reward fully justifies the incremental risk.

Even America's most successful investor, Warren Buffet, recommends that individual investors consider indexing. Investors would be wise to devote more attention to understanding the real advantages offered by the market fund—the powerful plodder.

---

[3]While there is some specialized evidence that quarterly earnings reports and information on "insider transactions" are not immediately and completely discounted in securities prices, the apparent opportunities to be exploited are so very limited that managers of large portfolios would not be able to make effective use of this kind of information anyway.

CHAPTER 4

THE PARADOX

APARADOX IS HAUNTING investment management.

The paradox is that funds with very long-term purposes are being managed to meet short-term objectives that may be neither feasible nor important. And they are *not* being managed to achieve long-term objectives that are both feasible and worthwhile.

The unimportant and difficult task to which most investment managers devote most of their time with little or no success is trying to "beat the market." Realistically—without taking above-average market risk—to outperform the equity market by even one half of 1 percent *consistently* would be a great success which almost no sizable investment managers have achieved for very long.

The truly important but not very difficult task to which investment managers and their clients could and should devote themselves involves four steps: (1) understanding the client's real needs, (2) defining realistic investment objectives that can meet a client's realistic needs, (3) establishing the right asset mix for each particular portfolio, and (4) developing well-reasoned, sensible investment policies designed to achieve the client's realistic and specified long-term investment objectives. In this work, success can be easily achieved.

For example, if the long-term average rate of return on bonds is 6 percent, and the return from investments in common stocks is 10 percent—because there must be a higher long-term rate of return on stocks to convince investors to accept the risk of equity investing—then shifting just 10 percent of the portfolio's assets from bonds to stocks and keeping it there would, over time, increase the portfolio's average annual rate of return by $^4/_{10}$ of 1 percent (4 percent higher return on stocks × 10 percent of assets = 0.40 percent).

Shifting the asset mix of a 60 percent equity/40 percent fixed-income portfolio to 70:30 may not be a major proposition, but, as noted in the previous chapter, consistently beating the market rate of return by 0.4 percentage points (or 40 basis points) a year through superior stock selection would be a substantial achievement.

The problem is not in the market, but in ourselves.

Very few professional investors have been able to sustain such superior results.

It is ironic that a change of even such modest magnitude in the basic asset allocation decision can capture an improvement in total return significantly greater than the elusive increment sought in the beat-the-market syndrome.

Clearly, if the asset mix truly appropriate to the client's objectives justified an even more substantial emphasis on equities—such as 80:20, or 90:10, or even 100:0—the incremental rate of return over the 60:40 portfolio would be even greater: 1.6 percent annually at 80:20 and 3.2 percent average annually at 100 percent. Virtually no large investment manager can hope to beat the market by such magnitudes.

Of course, these calculations are mechanical. They present averages ignoring the fact that actual returns in individual years come in an impressive, even alarming, distribution of actual annual returns around these averages.

The crucial question is not simply whether long-term returns on common stocks would exceed returns on bonds or bills *if* the investor held on through the many startling gyrations of the market.

The crucial question is whether the investor will, in fact, hold on for the long term so their expected average returns will be achieved. The problem is not in the market, but in ourselves, our perceptions, and our reactions to our perceptions.

During the 15 years from 1982 to 1997 mutual funds averaged approximately 15 percent in annual returns. However, mutual fund investors averaged only 10 percent. Why? Because instead of developing an astute long-term investing program and staying with it, investors jumped around from one fund to another. The result was the loss of a full one-third of the total returns earned by their funds—but *not* earned for themselves. This is why it is so important for each client to develop a realistic knowledge of his own or his organization's tolerance for market fluctuations and his long-term investment objectives, and to develop a realistic understanding of investing and of capital markets. The more you know about yourself as an investor and the more you understand investment management and the securities markets, the more you will know what asset mix is really right for your portfolios, and the more likely you will be able to sustain your commitment for the long term.

For investors, the real opportunity to achieve superior results is not in scrambling to outperform the market, but in establishing *and adhering to* appropriate investment policies over the long term—policies that position the portfolio to benefit from riding with the main long-term forces in the market. Investment policy, wisely formulated by realistic and well-informed clients with a long-term perspective and clearly defined objectives, is the foundation upon which portfolios should be constructed and managed over time and through market cycles.

In reality, very few investors have developed such investment policies. And because they have not, most investment managers are left to manage their clients' portfolios without knowing their clients' real objectives and without the discipline of explicit agreement on their mission as investment managers. *This is the client's fault.*

Investment policy is the foundation upon which portfolios should be constructed and managed.

As a result of not knowing enough about the particular facts and values of their different clients, investment managers typically manage all funds in virtually the same way and with very nearly the same asset mix, even in such extraordinarily different kinds of having an employee benefit funds as pension funds and profit-sharing funds.

The problem of a procrustean "one size fits all" asset mix is even more seriously worrisome when the clients are individuals. While most investment managers would, in theory, like to match the portfolios they manage to the specific needs and objectives of each particular client, the reality is that most managers work with a small number of standard asset mixes—and assign clients to these few alternatives. While the professionalism of investment counseling is more profound than the professionalism of managing investment portfolios—and can make far more economic difference to the client over the long term—most clients will neither do the disciplining work of formulating sound long-term investment policies for themselves nor pay sufficient fees to make counseling adequately rewarding for investment managers to provide this much more important service.

The profound differences between the functions and needs of pension plans and defined contribution 401(k) plans or profit-sharing plans make them striking examples of a disconcertingly standardized approach to the most important investment decision: the asset mix. So far as the total sum received by each individual is concerned, profit-sharing plans and 401(k) plans "terminate" entirely on the day he or she retires or leaves; thus the fund has a series of absolute and predictable end points.

This risk of "end-period dominance" calls for an investment policy that avoids major fluctuations in market value.[1] Pension plans, on the other hand, are virtually perpetual investment vehicles, funded to provide a stream of annuity payments to plan participants over a very long and highly predictable period; they can easily accept quite substantial market fluctuations during the long "interim" period.

That the investments of pension funds and profit sharing plans are not, in fact, differentiated on even such a powerful and basic dimension as the stock-bond ratio, leads to the sobering conclusion that while investment policy conforming to the client's particular investment objectives may be honored in theory, it is little used in practice.

Individual investors will want to learn from the mistakes of professional investors. Getting it right on investment policy is up to you the investor: after all, it's your money—so make it happen.

The differences among employee benefit plans can be substantial, but these differences will matter only if corporate executives vigorously represent the special characteristics of their company and their plan when basic investment policies are being formulated or reviewed.

It is hardly conceivable that senior corporate management would routinely delegate full operating responsibility for comparable millions of dol-

---

[1]Profit sharing plans can easily be designed to minimize this problem. In more and more companies, each plan participant has a separate account in which the asset mix can be adapted to the risk preferences of the individual and can be changed over time to reflect the worker's changing circumstances: all in growth stocks when young, shifting to a conservative balanced portfolio towards retirement, and so forth. Note, however, that shifting is probably not a good investment policy.

lars[2] to regular operating divisional executives—let alone a manager not directly supervised by top management—with only such broad guidelines or instructions as: "Try to do better than average," or "You're the experts, see what you can do for us." The same is just as true—and always will be true—for individual investors: Know what you really want.

The real question is not whether portfolio managers are constructing portfolios to match the goals and objectives of each specific client. (The uninspiring reality is that they do not.) The relevant question is: Who is responsible for bringing about the requisite change? The pragmatic answer is that the responsibility is not going to be fulfilled by investment managers. It will be left to the client. You can and should accept this responsibility.

You can do more for your portfolio's long-term rates of return by developing and sustaining wise long-range policies that commit you to an appropriate structure of investments than can be done by the most skillful manipulation of the individual holdings within the portfolio.

In brief, you should recognize that portfolio operations are subordinate to investment policy, and you should assert your responsibility for leadership in policy formation. This is not an investment problem that should be left to portfolio managers—no matter how skilled and conscientious they are—any more than, as Clemenceau observed, war should be left to the generals. It is your problem, and while responsibility for it can be abdicated, it really cannot be delegated.

Only you will know enough to speak with relevance and credibility to such important characteristics as the amount, timing, and certainty of flows *out* of the fund. Only the client knows his own (or his organization's) tolerance for changes in market prices—particularly at market extremes where it really matters—because it is at such stress periods when investment policies seem least certain and the pressure for change is most strong.

Individual investors will each know the most about their overall financial and investment situation—their earning power, their ability to save, their obligations for children's educational expenses, or the likely timing and scale of needs for spendable funds or how they feel about investments. College trustees will know the most about the linkages between the endowment and the annual budget or fund-raising.

---

[2]At some companies, pension fund assets are larger than the sponsoring corporation's net worth. For wealthy families, astute management of their existing portfolio of investments is clearly the most important dimension of their financial futures.

Corporate executives will know their pension plan's actuarial assumptions and how close to reality these assumptions really are; the company's tolerance for intrusions upon its quarter-to-quarter and year-to-year progression of reported earnings by a sudden need to fund a deficit in plan assets caused by an abrupt drop in their market value; the company's evolving philosophy of employee benefits and how benefit programs might be changed; the company's likelihood to increase benefits to retired plan participants to protect their purchasing power from the corrosion of inflation; and the tolerance of interim market fluctuations among staff, senior executives, and the board of directors. The "risk tolerance" of a corporate pension plan sponsor is not just the risk tolerance of the pension staff or even the senior financial officer: It is the risk tolerance of a majority of the board of directors at the moment of most severe market adversity.

Here are six important questions each client should think through, and then explain his own answers to the investment manager. (Investment managers would be wise to urge their clients to do this kind of "homework.")

First, what are the real risks of an adverse outcome, particularly in the short run? Unacceptable risks should never be taken. For example, it would not make sense to invest all of a high school senior's college tuition savings in the stock market because if the market went down, the student might not be able to pay the tuition bill. Nor would it make sense to invest money saved for a house in stocks just two or three years before the intended date of purchase.

Second, what are the probable emotional reactions of clients to an adverse experience? As the axiom goes, some investors care about *eating* well and some care about *sleeping* well. The portfolio manager should know and stay well within the client's informed tolerance for interim fluctuations in portfolio value. The emphasis on *informed tolerance* is deliberate. Avoidance of market risk does have a real "opportunity cost," and the client should be fully informed of the opportunity cost of each level of market risk *not* taken.

Third, how knowledgeable about investments and markets is the individual client or the institutional client's investment committee? Investing does not always "make sense" to the nonprofessional. Sometimes it seems almost perversely counterintuitive. Lack of knowledge tends to make investors too cautious during bear markets and too confident in bull markets—sometimes at considerable cost. Managers should be careful *not* to assume their clients are more sophisticated than they really are.

Portfolio managers can help their clients by explaining the way capital markets behave—and misbehave—and clients can help educate themselves about the differences between short-term experiences and long-term experiences.

The client who is very well informed about the investment environment will know what to expect. This client will be able to take in stride those disruptive experiences that may cause other less informed investors to overreact to either unusually favorable or unusually adverse market experience.

Fourth, what other capital or income resources does the client have and how important is the particular portfolio to the client's *overall* financial position? For example, pension funds sponsored by large and prosperous corporations can reasonably accept greater market risk than can a college endowment, which may have difficulty raising capital to replenish losses. A young business executive with a generous pension fund for safety can take greater short-term market risks. A retired widow usually cannot accept as much risk as can her alma mater.

Fifth, are any legal restrictions imposed on investment policy? Many personal trust funds are quite specific. Many endowment funds have restrictions that can be significant, particularly when they specify how income is to be defined or spent, or both.[3]

Sixth, are there any unanticipated consequences of interim fluctuations in portfolio value that might affect policy? A frequently cited example is the risk in a pension fund of being obliged to augment contributions if the portfolio's market value drops below a "trigger" level built into the actuaries' calculations of current contributions.[4] And we all know it can be very, very hard for individual investors to continue taking the very long-term view when markets are rising rapidly—or falling rapidly.

Each of these possible concerns should be rigorously examined to ascertain how much deviation from the normally optimal investment policy—broad diversification at a moderately above-average market risk—is truly warranted. Understanding and using these insights into the specific realities of the particular client's situation and objectives is the basis upon which wise investment policies should be developed for each different portfolio.

In pursuing the goal of developing and using wise investment policies, we must first recognize that most *institutional* funds such as pensions and

---

[3] As William Carey and Craig Bright advocate in their fine study, *The Law and the Lore of Endowment,* restrictions should be carefully examined because they may not be as confining as they might initially appear.

[4] Actuarial calculations have an apparent precision that Fellows of the Society of Actuaries would be among the first to caution are based on estimates and judgments.

endowments are *un*owned money: They do not really "belong" to anyone. There is no individual who can or would say "This is my money. *This* is what I want you to do with it. Or else." There are, in other words, no principals. On the other hand, with individual funds, the investor is the principal—and all too often is the "principal problem" because he wants to do something. Unfortunately, for the activist investor, history teaches that in investing patience and fortitude—or benign neglect—are more beneficial than activity. To rephrase the familiar admonition: "Don't just do something, stand there!"

Second, we should recognize that those who are "at the controls" at most institutional funds are usually only representatives of an organization and subject to after-the-fact criticism by powerful Monday-morning quarterbacks. These representatives have clear economic incentives to protect their careers: "It may not be my money, but it is my job and my career."

The careers of these institutional representatives seldom hinge on the work they do in setting investment policy or managing investment managers.

In such circumstances, what pattern of behavior would we expect of these representatives? Clearly they will be self-protective and defensive and will make their decisions with reference to a relatively short time period, say three to five years. They will not seek to optimize, they will seek the most acceptable near-term balance between desires for superior returns and avoidance of unusual or unorthodox positions. And above all, they will avoid any unnecessarily distressing risk to their own careers!

Investors must assert their role as experts on their own needs.

What are investment managers doing? The very same thing. They want to keep their accounts. They are understandably cautious, even too cautious. They are compromising with an overly defensive tilt, worrying too much about not losing the accounts they manage.

Observers of the paradox that haunts investment management say it is unrealistic to expect investment managers to risk strained client relationships by insisting on a well-conceived and carefully articulated investment policy with explicit objectives when their clients seem uninterested in going through the discipline.

For that, we must look not to the agents but to the principals. But in institutional investment management there *are* no principals. And all too few individual investors will assert themselves, assuming the professionals know more or know better. If investors are not willing to act like principals, then we can be sure that the paradox will remain for a long time. In this case, individual investors have an important opportunity to outperform institutional investors—by designing and deliberately achieving the optimal matchup between their real investment objectives and the long-term investment policy that's best for each of them. In other words, while you cannot beat the market, you can exploit the fact that so many others are trying to do so. By "looking the other way," you can focus on what really matters: not the futile struggle to beat the market, but the reasoned and highly achievable goal of setting, and meeting, your own long-term investment objectives. The more clearly you recognize that others are paying attention to the wrong thing, the more calmly and firmly you can pay attention to the right thing.

Escape from the paradox depends on clients asserting their role as experts on their own needs and resources and insisting on appropriate investment goals and policies.

5

TIME

TIME IS ARCHIMEDES' LEVER in investing.

Archimedes is often quoted as saying, "Give me a lever long enough and a place to stand, and I can move the earth." In investing, that lever is *time.* (And the place to stand, of course, is a firm and realistic investment policy.)

The length of time investments will be held, the period of time over which investment results will be measured and judged, is the single most powerful factor in any investment program.

If time is *short,* the highest return investments—the ones a long-term investor naturally most wants to own—will be undesirable, and the wise short-term investor will avoid them. But if the time period for investing is abundantly *long,* the wise investor can commit without great anxiety to investments that appear in the short run to be very risky.

Given enough time, investments that might otherwise seem unattractive may become highly desirable. Time transforms investments from *least* attractive to *most* attractive—and vice versa—because, while the average expected rate of return is not at all affected by time, the range or distribution of *actual* returns around the expected average is very greatly affected by time. The longer the time period over which investments are held, the closer the actual returns in a *portfolio*[1] will come to the expected average.

---

[1]The actual returns on *individual* investments will, in contrast, be more and more widely dispersed as the time period lengthens.

As a result, time changes the ways in which different kinds of investments can best be used by different investors with different situations and objectives.

The conventional time period over which rates of return are calculated—their average *and* their distribution—is one year. While convenient and widely used, this particular 12-month time frame simply does not match the time available to all the different kinds of investors with all their different constraints and purposes. For example, some investors are investing for only a few days at a time while other investors will hold their investments for several decades. And it is the difference in time horizon that really matters.

To show how important time really is, let's exaggerate for effect, and look at the returns expected in a *one-day* investment in common stocks.

Short-term risk should not be
a major concern to long-term investors.

The typical stock's share price is $40, and the range of trading during the day might easily be from 39¼ to 40½—a range of 1¼ or 3.1 percent of the average price for the day. Remembering that in today's market—with today's expectations for future inflation—the average annual rate of return for common stocks has been approximately 15 percent, let's postulate that an investment in this hypothetical stock would have an expected daily return of 0.06 percent (15 percent annual return divided by 250 trading days) and a range around that expected average of plus or minus 1.55 percent (3.1 percent intraday range divided by two).

Now, let's "annualize" that daily return of 0.06 percent and that 3.1 percent daily variation. The average annual expected rate of return would be 15 percent, but the *range* of returns around the 15 percent would be a daunting ±387.5 percent! (In other words, the annual rate of return for a one-day investment in our hypothetical stock would be somewhere between a *profit* of 405.5 percent and a *loss* of 372.5 percent!)

Of course, no sensible investor would knowingly invest in common stocks only for a single day or month or even for a year. Such brief time periods are clearly too short for investments in common stocks, because the expectable *variation* in return is too large in comparison to the average expected return. The extra uncertainty incurred when investing in common stocks is not balanced by a sufficiently large or sufficiently sure reward.

Such short-term holdings in common stocks are not investments: They are rank speculations.

On the other hand, this deliberate one-day burlesque of the conventional use of annual rates of return leads to a serious examination of the differences in investor satisfaction when the measurement period is changed. And this examination shows why an investor with a very *long* time horizon might well invest entirely in common stocks just as wisely as another investor with a very *short* time horizon would invest only in Treasury bills or a money market fund. The examination also shows why an intermediate-term investor would, as his time horizon extended outward, shift investment emphasis from money market instruments toward bonds and then toward more and more equities.

Time transforms certain investments
from *least* attractive to *most* attractive—
and vice versa.

Both the constancy of the average *expected* rate of return—no matter what the time period—and the profound impact of time on the actual realized rate of return is clearly demonstrated in the charts in Figure 5-1.

The one-year-at-a-time rates of return on common stocks over the years are almost incoherent. They show both large and small gains and large and small losses occurring in what appears to be a random pattern. At best, you could have earned 4 percent in a year; but at worst you could have lost 37.4 percent. It seems absurd to "summarize" those wildly disparate one-year experiences as having any "average" rate of return.

Shifting to five-year periods brings a considerable increase in coherence or regularity. There are, for example, *few* periods with losses, and the periods with gains appear far more *often* and consistently. The reason is that as the measurement period lengthens, the average rate of return begins to overpower the single year differences.

Shifting once again to 10-year periods increases the consistency of returns significantly. Only *one* loss is experienced and most periods show average annual gains of 5 to 15 percent. Again, the power of the average rate of return—now compounded over a decade—overwhelms the single year differences.

Moving on to 20-year periods brings even more consistency to the experienced rate of return. There are no losses, only gains. And the gains

FIGURE 5-1   Range of returns for stocks, bonds, and cash after inflation (1901–1990)

Courtesy of Cambridge Associates.

Stocks

	1-Year Periods	5-Year Periods	10-Year Periods	15-Year Periods	20-Year Periods	25-Year Periods
High	53.37%	28.98%	17.86%	14.63%	13.03%	11.50%
Average	8.26%	6.51%	6.08%	6.02%	6.22%	6.57%
Low	−37.35%	−11.65%	−3.89%	−1.57%	0.78%	2.73%

Bonds

	1-Year Periods	5-Year Periods	10-Year Periods	15-Year Periods	20-Year Periods	25-Year Periods
High	37.15%	18.99%	9.91%	10.17%	8.64%	6.47%
Average	2.36%	2.02%	1.61%	1.45%	1.51%	1.60%
Low	−19.75%	−10.44%	−5.21%	−3.87%	−2.68%	−1.77%

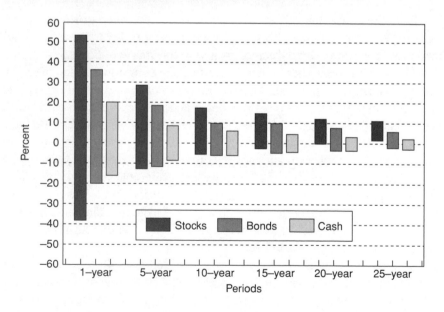

cluster more closely together around the long-term expected average rate of return.

Despite the obviously substantial differences in the range or distribution of returns in each time frame, there is one central constant: the *average* actual rate of return is almost the same in all cases. This is because the data shown are all samples from the same continuous stream of investment experience.

Appreciating that actual experiences in investing are samples drawn from a continuous stream of experience is vital to understanding the meaning contained in the data. Even in New England, the weather—when considered over a long period of time—becomes a sensible, reliable *climate* even though the days of bitter cold or sweltering heat seem individually so unpredictable, particularly as to the exact date of occurrence. Similarly, in investing, the patient observer can see the true underlying patterns that make the seemingly random year-by-year or month-by-month or day-by-day experiences not disconcerting or confusing, but rather splendidly predictable—on average and over time.

In weather and investments, larger and more numerous samples enable us to come closer and closer to understanding the normal experience from which the sample is drawn. It is this understanding of the normal experience that enables us to design our own behavior so we can take advantage of the dominant normal pattern over the long term and not be thrown off by the confusing daily events that present themselves with such force in the short term.

The single most important dimension of investment policy is asset mix, particularly the ratio of fixed-income investments to equity investments.

Discussions of asset mix have attracted considerable attention in recent years, particularly among pension managers. Their analyses show that over and over again the trade-off between risk and reward is driven by one key factor: time.

Unfortunately, in most cases the time horizon being used is not chosen for the specific fund but is instead a conventional five years. A five-year "horizon" usually leads to the familiar 60:40 ratio of equities to debt. A 10-year horizon leads to an 80:20 ratio. A 15-year horizon typically results in a 90:10 ratio. And so it goes. The unfortunate reality is that none of these time horizons is "right" for a pension fund or a university endowment or even for most individual investors. They are all far too short for a fund with an investment horizon of 30 to 50 years or even more.

What is most disturbing about asset mix decisions is not that they are made with an inappropriately short time horizon, but that there is almost no evidence that such decisions are made deliberately and explicitly. For example, there is no evidence of differences in asset mix between such obviously different employee benefit plans as pension plans and profit sharing plans. Nor are there significant differences among pension plans with such obvious differentiations as companies with high actuarial rate-of-return assumptions versus companies with low actuarial rate-of-return assumptions; companies with an old work force versus companies with a young work force; companies with fast growth in earnings versus companies with little or no growth in earnings; or by the percent of fund obligations now funded or by the percent of corporate profits being paid into the plan as annual contributions.

The irony is that while their nearly perpetual character enables pension funds to accept interim market risk better than any other type of investor, the typical pension fund was, in the 1970s, 1980s, and 1990s, only 50 percent in equities. In other words, the time horizon actually being used in managing the typical pension fund was not 30 years or 50 years, but only three or four.

These funds paid an opportunity cost in returns forgone. As it turned out, the cost of not being fully invested in stocks in the 1980s and 1990s was *very* large: equities produced record returns, an astounding 17 percent *compounded!* Investment history documents conclusively (as seen in Chapter 2) that the very first weeks of a market recovery produce a substantial proportion of the gains to be experienced. Yet, it is at the crucial market bottom that the market timer is most likely to be out of the market—missing "the best part."[2] But that is not the point at issue here. The point is investors should have taken such a cautious asset mix decision only after examining the inherent risks and rewards and deciding what policy would be best for them. Such powerful decisions should be made deliberately and only after careful examination of long-term realities.

Recognizing that taking the very long-term view is easier with institutional funds than for individuals, it is clear that if more investors insisted on such long-range policy reviews, their funds would typically be invested differently and would earn higher returns.

[2]Robert H. Jeffrey, "The Folly of Stock Market Timing," *Harvard Business Review,* July–August, 1984.

6

RETURNS

INVESTMENT RETURNS COME, as everyone knows, in two very different forms: quite predictable cash received from interest or dividends; and gains or losses in market price that are, particularly in the short run, quite *un*predictable. Investors devote most of their time and skill trying to increase returns from changes in market prices—by outsmarting each other. They are making a big mistake.

Changes in market price are caused by changes in the consensus of active investors of what the price of a stock ought to be. This consensus is determined by thousands and thousands of institutions and individuals constantly seeking opportunities for investment profit. To find these opportunities, investors study monetary and fiscal economics and political developments in all the major nations; visit hundreds and hundreds of companies; attend thousands of breakfast, lunch, and dinner meetings with corporate executives, economists, industry experts, securities analysts, and other experts; study reports and analyses produced in enormous volume by hundreds of companies and dozens of large brokerage firms; read extensively in the industry and trade press; and talk almost constantly on the telephone with people who have ideas, information, or insights with which these active investors might improve their investment performance.

In addition to studying the *rational* world, investors also study the irrational world of "investor psychology," public confidence, politics, and "market tone," because in the short run the markets—and market prices—are very human or nonrational. The ways in which investors perceive and interpret information and the ways they react to developments have great impact on market prices, particularly in the short run. So active investors are always looking for opportunities to capitalize on changes in other investors' opinions before changes in their own opinions are capitalized on by other investors. Not all of the investors' interpretations and perceptions are "correct." Many, particularly in retrospect, seem very wrong.

Investment management in today's dynamic markets is a wonderful, turbulent, fascinating, hopeful, anguishing, stressful, and euphoric process of competing in the world's most free and competitive market against many talented and ambitious competitors for advantage gained from greater knowledge and wiser interpretation and better timing. (The irony is that for most investment managers and their clients most of this activity really does not matter—not because these investment managers are not talented, but because so many of their competitors are *equally* talented. It's not how good you are that counts, but how good you are compared with your competitors.)

For all the surface complexity in the process, two main areas are dominant in the evaluation of common stocks. The first is the general consensus of investors on the probable amount and timing of future earnings and dividends. The second is the consensus of investors on the discount rate at which this stream of estimated future dividends and earnings should be capitalized to establish its present value.

The consensus estimates of future dividends and earnings will vary among different investors and at different times due to changes in expectations for secular growth and cyclical fluctuations in unit demand; prices and taxes; discoveries and inventions; changes in the competition at home and abroad, and so forth. And over time, the discount rate considered appropriate will vary with many factors, among which the most important will be the perceived risk of the particular investment or investments of its general type and the expected rate of inflation and the discount factor that converts a stream of expected future payments in dividends or interest to that present capital value.

It's not how good you are that counts, but how good you are compared with your competitors.

The longer the future period over which estimates—both of earnings and dividends and of the discount rate—must be extended, the greater the day-to-day or month-to-month fluctuations in the stock price that will be caused by changes in the investors' consensus of present value. But, as everyone knows, price and value are not the same thing.

The average long-term experience in investing is *never* surprising, but the short-term experience is *always* surprising.

As the time horizon over which an estimate extends is lengthened, the impact of the estimated discount rate becomes more and more dominant (relative to estimates of future earnings and dividends) on the current market price of a security.

For investment value, on the other hand, as the holding period over which the investor owns an investment lengthens, the importance of the discount factor decreases and the importance of the dividends paid increases.

For the very long-term *investor* who cares about value, the relative importance of earnings and dividends received is overwhelming. For the very short-term *speculator* who cares about price, everything depends on the day-to-day and month-to-month changes in investor psychology (or in more formal terms, the appropriate discount rate) and what people are willing to pay. Like the weather, the average long-term experience in investing is never surprising, but the short-term experience is *always* surprising.

The history of returns on investment, as documented in study after study, shows three basic characteristics:

1. Common stocks have average returns higher than bonds, which in turn have higher returns than short-term money market instruments.

2. The daily, monthly, and yearly fluctuations in actual returns on common stocks exceed the fluctuations in returns on bonds, which in turn exceed the fluctuations on short-term money market instruments.

3. The magnitude of the period-to-period fluctuation in rate of return increases as the measurement period is shortened and decreases as the measurement period is lengthened. In other words, rates of return appear more normal over long periods of time.

The really impressive characteristic of investment returns is that the *variation* in year-to-year rates of return on common stocks dwarfs the average annual rate of return on stocks.

We now know that it is nonsense to say, "Common stocks have produced an average rate of return of 9 percent." This is an incomplete and misleading statement. Far better, we could say, "Over the past 50 years, the actual returns have been between a *loss* of 43 percent,[1] and a *gain* of 54 percent. While the geometric mean rate of return is about 9 percent, the standard deviation of actual returns around that mean is nearly 22 percent. And finally, we regret to say we cannot give you the sequence with which those returns will be experienced. They, of course, occur at random."

The two statements are remarkably different from one another—particularly for the investor who is suddenly and unexpectedly experiencing the most dreadfully negative year in what was so serenely described as the "normal" bell-shaped distribution. That's why institutional investors and investment managers are learning to describe investment returns in formal statistical terms. Individual investors would be well advised to learn enough about the useful language of statistics to have an appreciative awareness of what is meant by *mean* and *bell curve* or *normal distribution* and what is meant by *two standard deviations* as a measure of the frequency with which unusual events *are* expected and *do* occur.

In addition to learning the importance of describing the distribution of returns around that mean, we have also learned to separate out the different components in the average rate of return and to analyze each component separately.

There are three main components in the average rate of return:

1. The *real* risk-free rate of return before adjusting for inflation.[2]
2. A premium over the risk-free rate of return to offset the expected erosion of purchasing power due to inflation.
3. A premium over the inflation-adjusted risk-free rate of return to compensate investors for accepting market risk.

Dividing total returns into these three classes of return makes it possible to compare the returns of each type of investment—stocks, bonds, and bills. This work has been done in a series of landmark studies by Roger Ibbotson and Rex Sinquefield, and the accompanying table from their book shows their major findings for the 55-year period 1926–91 (see Figure 6-1). The analysis is very informative.[3]

[1]These rates of return are normal (or pre-inflation) while the data cited on pages 33–34 are "real" (after being corrected for inflation).

[2]There is no risk of default in a Treasury bill because if the government were short of money it would simply print more!

[3]Roger G. Ibbotson and Rex A. Sinquefield, *Stocks, Bonds, Bills, and Inflation: The Past and the Future* (Charlottesville, Va.: Financial Analysts Research Foundation, 1982).

**FIGURE 6-1   Wealth indexes of investments in the U.S. Capital Markets
1925–1990 (year-end 1925 = 1.00)**

Source: Stocks, Bonds, Bills, and Inflation 1991 Yearbook, *Copyright © 1984–1991 Ibbotson Associates, Inc. All Rights Reserved. Stocks, Bonds, and Inflation and SBBI are service marks of Ibbotson Associates.*

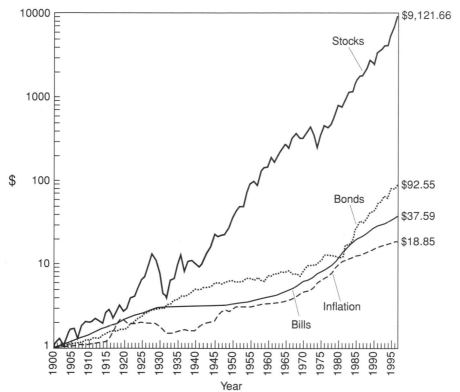

Treasury bills appear quite safe and reliable—in nominal terms, not
adjusted for inflation—with apparently positive returns in 54 of 55 years.
However, when adjusted for inflation, returns are positive just less than 60
percent of the time: Even more startling, the average annual rate of return
on bills, after adjusting for inflation, is zero.

In other words, Treasury bills are usually no more than a match for
inflation. Most of the time, you do get your money back—with its purchasing power intact. But that is all you get. There is virtually no real return *on*
your money, just the return *of* your money.

Long bonds produce higher returns, inflation adjusted, for two reasons: corporate bonds involve a risk of default; and both corporate and government bonds impose on the investor an exposure to market fluctuations due to their more distant maturity and investors "adjusting" to changing interest rates. Investors don't want such market price fluctuations unless they get a higher rate of return to compensate, so long bonds pay a higher rate of interest—a *maturity premium*. The maturity premium is estimated at 0.9 percent and the default premium on high-grade long-term corporate bonds works out at 0.5 percent. Adding these two premiums to the risk-free rate, the inflation-adjusted annual real rate of return on long government bonds is 1.0 percent and on long corporates, about 1.4 percent.

Similarly, the risk premium on common stocks is calculated at 6.1 percent. (The inflation-adjusted expected *real* rate of return is, congruently, the same: 6.1 percent.)

When the powerfully disruptive impact of inflation is removed, and when return experience is examined in reasonably long time periods, it becomes clear how consistent investment returns (or the returns investors require for their money) really are.

This consistency stems from two main factors:

1.   Investors are sensibly consistent in requiring higher rates of return to compensate them for accepting higher market risk.

2.   As the period over which returns are measured is lengthened, the short-term volatility in returns caused by changes in the discount rate becomes less and less important and the expected dividend stream, which is more stable, becomes more and more important.

The central point is that we do not have and cannot hope to get perfectly precise or "correct" data on rates of return from investments in securities—any more than we can expect to get "correct" data by sampling any other complex, dynamic, continuous process, impacted by a multitude of large and small exogenous factors. However, we can get a very useful *approximation* of what returns have actually been and what they are most likely to be—and that is all we really need to establish basic investment policies for the long term.

Unless you buy in at the start of the period measured, sell out at the end, and take your money out of the market, performance data are simply hypothetical statistics. They describe samples from a continuous and very long-term process in which stock prices go through a "random walk" series of successive approximations of the actual present value of each stock based on continuously revised estimates of future earnings dividends and frequently changed discount rates.

Two further propositions on returns are important. First, the impact on returns of changes in the expected level of inflation can be enormous, particularly on common stocks which are virtually perpetuities. Such a change in the expected rate of inflation from approximately 2 percent in 1960 to approximately 10 percent in 1980 (along with other changes) caused a change in the required nominal average rate of return from common stocks from about 9 percent in 1960 to about 17 percent in 1980, and this produced a major reduction in stock prices. Inflation adjusted, the loss investors experienced during the adjustment was the worst in half a century.

A further increase in the expected rate of inflation would have further depressed stock prices. This would drop stock prices down to the level from which buyers would get sufficient returns—with the same future "real" earnings and dividends as previously expected—to offset the now expected rate of inflation, compensate for risk, and provide a risk-free real rate of return of about 6 percent plus or minus 12 percent in two out of three years. A decrease in the expected rate of inflation would have the opposite effect, as we saw in 1982 and the following 15 years.

The second proposition on returns is that differences in rates of return that may appear moderate in the short run can, with compounding, multiply into very large and quite obvious differences in the long run. (When asked what he considered man's most powerful discovery, Albert Einstein replied without hesitation: "Compound interest!")[4]

When asked what he considered man's most powerful discovery, Albert Einstein replied without hesitation: "Compound interest."

The following table shows the compounding effect on $1.00 invested at different compound rates compounded over different periods of time (see Figure 6-2). It's well worth careful study—particularly to see how powerful is *time*. That's why time is the "Archimedes' lever" of investment management.

[4]Compounding means you not only receive interest on your principal, but also interest on your reinvested interest.

FIGURE 6-2   Compound interest over time

Investment Period

Compound Rate of Return	5 Years	10 Years	20 Years
4%	$1.22	$1.48	$2.19
6	1.34	1.79	2.65
8	1.47	2.16	4.66
10	1.61	2.59	6.73
12	1.76	3.11	9.65
14	1.93	3.71	13.74
16	2.10	4.41	19.46
18	2.29	5.23	27.39
20	2.49	6.19	38.34

7

RISK

R*ISK* **IS SUCH A SIMPLE** little word that it is amazing how many different meanings are given to it by different users. (Risk is different from uncertainty: *Risk* describes the expected payoffs when their probabilities of occurrence are knowable. Actuarial mortality tables are a familiar example. The actuary does *not* know what will happen in 14 years to Mr. Frank Smith, but *does* know quite precisely what to expect for a group of 100 million people *as a group*—in *each* year—including the 14th year.) *Riskiness* is akin to *uncertainty* in investing—and that's what the academics mean when discussing beta and "risk." Too bad they don't use the exact terms.

Active investors typically think of risk in four different ways. One is price risk: You can lose money by buying stock at too high a price, and if you think a stock *might* be high, you know you are taking some price risk.

Another type of risk is called interest rate risk: If interest rates go up—to offset a change in expectations for inflation—more than is now expected (and already discounted in the market), your stocks will go down. You'll know you were taking risk.

A third type of risk is business risk. The company may blunder and earnings may not develop. If so, the stock will drop. Again you were taking risk.

In the extreme, the company may fail completely. That's what happened with Equity Funding, Penn Central, and Baring Brothers, and very nearly happened with IBM. As the old pros will tell you, "Now *that* is *risk!*"

They are right. But there is another way to look at risk that has come from the extensive academic research done over the past three decades;

more and more investment managers and clients are using it, because there's nothing so powerful as a theory that works. Here's the concept:

> Investors are exposed to three kinds of investment risk. One kind of risk simply *cannot be avoided,* but investors are rewarded for taking it. Two other kinds of risk *can be avoided* or even *eliminated,* and investors are not rewarded for accepting these unnecessary and avoidable kinds of risk.

Before exploring these three quite different kinds of risk more fully— and showing how investment managers and clients can use their understanding to establish investment policy—let's pause to show the way active investors think about risk of the kind we'll soon see is *not* rewarded.

The basic assumption of all active investors is that they will do better than the market because they will discover and exploit opportunities for profit by buying stocks that are underpriced or by selling stocks or groups of stocks that are overpriced.

For active investors, the risk they take that their judgment will prove wrong is a cost they are willing to incur as they reach out for opportunity. They do not expect to be right all the time, but they certainly expect to have a good batting average. (As explained in Chapter 1, most will be disappointed.) What is important at this point in our discussion is that active investors should not expect to profit *because* they take risks on individual stocks or groups of stocks: They should expect to profit *in spite of* the risks taken (after compensating for their losses or errors).

Now let's return to the theory that is so powerful and useful. As noted, investors are exposed to three kinds of investment risk. One kind of risk simply cannot be avoided, but it does pay investors for taking it. Two other kinds of risk can be virtually eliminated, and do not pay the person who takes them.

The risk that cannot be avoided is the risk inherent in the overall market. This market risk pervades all investments. It can be increased by selecting volatile securities or by using leverage, and it can be decreased by selecting securities with low volatility or by keeping part of a portfolio in cash equivalents. But it cannot be avoided or eliminated. It is always there. So it must be *managed.*

The two kinds of risk that can be avoided or eliminated are closely associated. One involves the risk linked to individual securities; the other involves the risk that is common to a group of securities. The first can be called individual stock risk, and the second can be called stock group risk.[1]

A few examples will clarify the meaning of stock group risk. Growth stocks will, as a group, move up and down in price in part because of changes in investor confidence and willingness to look more or less distantly into the future. (When investors are very confident, they will look far into the future when evaluating growth stocks.) Interest-sensitive issues such as utility and bank stocks will all be affected by changes in expected interest rates. Stocks in the same industry—autos, retailers, computers, and so forth—will share market price behavior driven by changing expectations for their industry as a whole. The number of common causes that affect groups of stocks is surely great, and most stocks belong simultaneously to several different groups. To avoid unnecessary complexity, and to avoid triviality, portfolio managers will usually focus their thinking on major forms of stock group risk.

There are three kinds of investment risk. Two can be virtually eliminated. The third, market risk, must be managed.

The central fact about both stock group risk and individual stock risk is this: They *do not need to be accepted* by the investor. They can be eliminated. Unlike the risk of the overall market, risk that comes from investing in particular market segments or specific issues can be diversified away—to oblivion.

As a result, in an efficient market no incremental reward can or will be earned over the market rate of return simply by taking either more individual stock risk or more stock group risk. Either type of risk should be incurred only when doing so will enable the portfolio manager to make an investment that will achieve truly worthwhile increases in returns. The evi-

---

[1]Academic writers use slightly different terms to describe the same three types of risk: market risk is called *systematic risk,* individual stock risk is *specific risk,* and stock group risk is *extra market risk.* The terms used here seem clearer and more natural. Risk identified as either individual stock risk or stock group risk is the risk that the *price* of an individual stock or group of stocks will behave differently than the overall market—either favorably or unfavorably—over the time period for which investment returns are measured.

dence is overwhelming that, while enticing, such ventures are not sufficiently rewarding. Yes, professional investors are often quoted as being
"overweighted" in one group or another, but the reality that this is being
done does not mean it is, on average, successful.

The lack of reward for taking individual stock risk or stock group risk
is important because the portfolio manager who takes such risks with his
clients' funds can only hope to be rewarded by his superior skill—relative
to the aggregate skill of all competing investment managers—in selecting
individual stocks or groups of stocks that were inappropriately priced. As
explained in Chapter 2, the investment manager who takes these risks can
only profit if his competitors have made mistakes.

By assuming greater-than-average market risk, investors can earn greater-than-average returns.

Clearly, such risks can be avoided by the simple and convenient strategy of designing a portfolio that replicates the market: no deviations in
portfolio composition, no deviations in rate of return relative to the overall
market, and no stock group risk or individual stock risk.

Note that eliminating these two particular forms of risk does not mean
all risk is gone. Overall market risk will always be there, and in the field of
risk, that's the big one.

The great advantage of an index fund, a portfolio that replicates the
overall market, is this: Such a fund provides a convenient and inexpensive
way to invest in equities, with the riskiness of particular market segments
and specific issues diversified away.

Risk-averse investors are willing to accept lower rates of return if they
can reduce the market risks they *must* take in investing. And they are willing to see other investors get higher rates of return as an inducement to
accept a larger share of the unavoidable market risk. But they will not pay
their risk-taking confreres to take risks that can quite easily be avoided alto-
gether by "buying the market."

Market risk is different. Because it cannot be eliminated, risk-averse
investors must and will accept a less-than-market rate of return in order to
achieve a less-than-market risk. And by so doing, they proffer an above-
average rate of return to investors willing to accept a greater-than-average
market risk. This is why investors who accept more-than-average market

risk—particularly over time—are rewarded with better-than-average market returns. (Recently, another very different kind of market risk has become a source of real concern. Overall, the stock market has risen so much that there may be an unusual, but very daunting, risk in the level of the whole market.)

The level of market risk taken in an equity portfolio can be estimated with good accuracy by calculating the historical price behavior of the stocks in the portfolio (on a weighted average) relative to changes in the market as a whole.[2]

The optimal level of market risk—for the very long-term investor—is moderately above the average. This level makes sense because many other investors are not free to take a very long-term view; their investments will be liquidated sooner—for children's education or at the termination of a trust or for a host of other near-to-medium-term events for which plans must be made. Other investors are simply unable to look with calm forebearance on the abrupt and substantial day-to-day, month-to-month, and year-to-year changes in stock prices that will be experienced in an equity portfolio over the long term. These investors want less risk and less fluctuation—and are willing to pay a price to get what they want.

In summary, the total return to an equity investor has four components: (1) the risk-free return; (2) an extra return to compensate for the riskiness or price uncertainty of investing in the overall equity market; (3) a potential extra return for investing in one or more particular groups of stocks or market segments that for various economic, business, or market psychology reasons might behave differently from the overall market; (4) a potential extra return for investing in specific stocks that, for the same sorts of reasons, might behave differently from the overall market.

In a similar manner, the risk accepted by the portfolio can be separated into the same kinds of component parts: risk associated with emphasis on specific stocks; risk associated with emphasis on or avoidance of particular groups of stocks or market segments that are influenced in similar ways by common causes; and risk associated with investing in equities per se.

---

[2]The market risk inherent in investing in any one market can, of course, be reduced in a multimarket portfolio by balancing investments in one market with investments in other markets that behave differently. This sort of diversification is an important motivation behind the interest in investing in real estate and in diversifying internationally. The stock markets of France, Hong Kong, Japan, Italy, and Australia fluctuate as much or more than the American market, but usually at different times and for somewhat different reasons. The multimarket portfolio with its investment in several different markets will have reduced the "unavoidable" market risk of any one market.

So, corresponding to each component of *return*—except the risk-free return—is a component of *risk*. Total risk consists of an overall equity market component plus a market segment risk plus a risk related to uncertainty about the price behavior of the stocks of individual companies relative to the overall market.

Market segment risk and specific issue risk can be diversified away, as explained above, but overall equity market risk cannot. Figure 7-1 shows vividly how the riskiness of a single stock consists primarily of specific issue risk and market segment risk, but that in a typical portfolio, these two kinds of risk are reduced to only a small part of the investor's total risk.

The chart also shows that the typical large pension fund with several different managers will have even more diversification and that this surfeit of diversification will further reduce the specific issue and market segment risks to a very small percentage of total risk.

FIGURE 7-1   How diversification reduces nonmarket risk

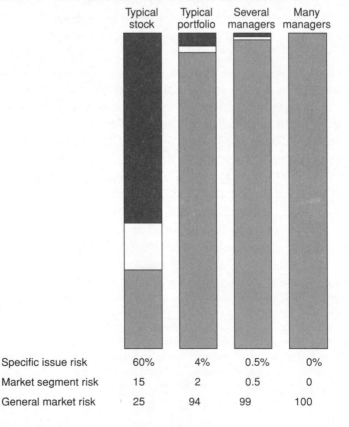

	Typical stock	Typical portfolio	Several managers	Many managers
Specific issue risk	60%	4%	0.5%	0%
Market segment risk	15	2	0.5	0
General market risk	25	94	99	100

This phenomenon of very great diversification so often experienced in large funds employing several managers—usually with each manager chosen specifically because of his or her "different" style of investing, but with their differences tending to cancel each other out—raises serious questions about very active management in institutional investing versus passive management with above-average market risk.

In investment management, we now know that the crucial factor is not how to manage rates of return, but rather how to manage market risk. By managing market risk, we mean doing two things at the same time: (1) deciding deliberately what level of market risk to establish as the portfolio's basic policy, and (2) holding to that chosen level of market risk. Changes in the level of market risk should only be made when there has been a deliberate change in basic, long-term investment policy.

Managing market risk is the primary objective of investment management.

With market risk under control, you can decide whether and when to accept any individual stock risks or stock group risks in order to capture extra profits. Note that while this part of investment management gets most of the attention by far from investors it is usually only a side show compared to the main force driven by the chosen level of market risk.

That managing market risk is the primary objective of investment management is a profound assertion. It is the core idea of this entire chapter. The rate of return obtained in an investment portfolio comes from three sources, in this order of importance: first and foremost, the level of market risk assumed—or avoided—in the portfolio; next, the consistency with which that risk level is maintained through market cycles; and last, the skill with which specific stock risk and stock group risk are eliminated or minimized through portfolio diversification or are well rewarded when deliberately taken.

The difference between true investment risk and apparent riskiness or market risk is a function of time. Yes, stocks can be very risky if time is short. But unless you begin your investment program at a seriously "too high" level in the stock market, when time is long enough, the *apparent* riskiness of stocks evaporates and the favorable long-term returns become increasingly evident—as in Figure 7-2. For investors, the risk in investing can be divided by *time* into short-term risk and long-term risk.

The real risk in the short term is that the investor will need to sell—to raise cash—when the market just happens to be low. That's why, in the *long*

FIGURE 7-2   The longer you hold stocks, the less your risk, the surer your gain . . .

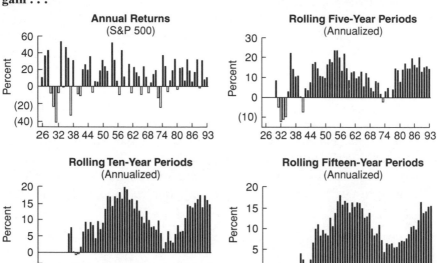

term, the risks are clearly *lowest* for stocks, but in the *short* term, the risks are just as clearly *highest* for stocks. (If you do not need to sell and don't sell, you really shouldn't much care about the nominal fluctuations of stock prices. They may be interesting, but they aren't any more relevant to you than is stormy weather in faraway places or low tide on the high seas.) And as we've already seen, the real risks in the long run are the risks of inflation and excessive caution.

To the extent you know your investments will be held for the very long term, you have automatically self-insured against the uncertainty of short-term market price fluctuations, because so long as you stay invested, the fluctuations just won't matter at all. The investor's best answer to short-term market riskiness is to ignore the interim fluctuations and be a long-term investor.

Recognition that risk drives returns instead of being simply a residual of the struggle for higher returns transforms the concept of investment policy.[3] We now know to focus not on rate of return but on the informed management of risk.

---

[3] As a child, I assumed the pendulum in the grandfather's clock was driving the minute and hour hands *forward* rather than, as I later learned, holding the hands back and controlling the rate at which the weights could move them forward. For me, the concept of a clock will never be the same.

C H A P T E R 8

BUILDING PORTFOLIOS

WHETHER INVESTMENT MANAGEMENT is primarily art or science has long been a favorite topic of informal discussion among professional investment managers, perhaps because the discussions are typically resolved quite cheerfully by demonstrating that since the practice of investment management is clearly not a science, it must therefore be an art.

Anyone who has observed gifted investors at work will recognize the art—subtle, intuitive, complex, and usually quite inexplicable—in selecting individual stocks or groups of stocks. The great artists are true heroes of the profession—Phil Fisher, John Neff, Peter Lynch, John Templeton, George Soros, Parker Hall, Warren Buffett, and Rowe Price. These unusually talented investors—and others—add value to portfolios by seeing and seizing opportunities others miss or recognize only later. For these paragons, there is art in stock picking.

But for most investment managers, portfolio management is neither art nor science. It is instead a very special problem in engineering, of determining the most reliable and efficient way of reaching a specified goal, given a set of policy constraints, and working within a remarkably uncertain, probabilistic, always changing world of partial information and *mis*information, all filtered through the inexact filter of human interpretation.

While certainly far from perfect, recent advances in the availability of data and the development of modern portfolio theory are providing investment managers—and their more sophisticated clients—with the tools and analytical frames of reference they need to understand and define the investment problem so it can be managed. (It would be a naive presumption to believe that the problems of managing an investment portfolio can be "solved." We must be willing to live with their being brought under reasonable control and being managed to a satisfactory standard of performance.)

An efficient portfolio maximizes expected returns at a deliberately chosen level of market risk.

As explained in Chapter 6, we now know that the real challenge in portfolio management is not how to increase *returns*—by buying low and selling high—but how to *manage risk* by deliberately taking appropriate risks or bets that lead predictably over time to increased returns.

The distinctive characteristic of effective portfolio management is the elimination of *unintended* risk associated with individual stocks or groups of stocks and the deliberate assumption of intended market risk.

While it is possible to add value through brilliant stock picking, investments in individual stocks and bonds are best thought of as components to be used in building a well-designed portfolio. They may be good components or poor components, but in the context of portfolio management, individual securities have value only to the extent they enable the investment manager to improve the portfolio as a whole by increasing the return or reducing risk or both. Portfolio management is investment engineering.

In line with the concept of portfolio management as a challenge in engineering, the portfolio design that eliminates avoidable and unintended risk and maximizes expected returns at a deliberately chosen level of market risk is an *efficient* portfolio. An efficient portfolio has greater expected return than any other feasible portfolio with equal risk, and less risk than any other feasible portfolio with equal expected return.

Once such an efficient portfolio has been constructed, it would not make sense to incur either individual stock risk or stock group risk unless such available risk were directly associated with—and judged worth taking in order to exploit—a specific opportunity to capture extra return.

The amount by which market risk and return can be magnified in a portfolio by investing in higher market risk—more volatile stocks—is not spectacular, but the benefits, over the very long run, can be worthwhile. A portfolio with a market risk that is 20 percent greater than the overall market average is feasible. A market risk much higher than that would be difficult to design into a portfolio and still have the portfolio well diversified. The number and variety of stocks needed to achieve good diversification and to provide that much market risk simply are not available in the market.

The expected "extra" rate of return for the portfolio with 20 percent more than average market risk would be, on average and over the very long term, 1.4 percentage points annually.[1] If 1.4 percentage points of incremental return over the market average return seems modest, remember that *no* sizable institutional investor has achieved that amount of annual incremental return over any sustained period of time!

Thus far, our discussion has concentrated on equity investments. Portfolio management for bonds is different in the details, but the main concepts are basically the same.

Like stocks, bonds present both individual bond risks and group risks. For example, bonds issued by companies in a particular industry will, as a group, change in value with major changes in that industry's economics. Bonds with particular call or refunding features in common will rise and fall as a group in relative market popularity. The normal difference in yield (and therefore price) between corporate and government bonds changes, causing larger or smaller spreads between corporates as a group and governments as a group.

It is important to note that bond rating agencies have found most of their rating errors caused by the difficulty inherent in estimating such group risks, not in estimating the individual risk of a particular issuer compared to other issuers in the same industry or group.

Bond portfolio management starts conceptually with a passive portfolio that represents the overall bond market. This baseline portfolio will be diversified across numerous issues to protect against the credit risk of individual issuers and will use a defensive, evenly spaced schedule of maturities to defend against adverse changes in interest rates. The overall quality of the portfolio and its average maturity will be set in concert with the client's risk preferences and potential liquidity needs.

---

[1] Calculated as follows: 1.2 × 7 percent return on equities over and above the risk-free rate of return = 1.4 percent incremental return.

As with equities, the historical evidence is that the risk of individual bonds can be substantially eliminated through diversification with the result that portfolios of medium-to-lower-grade issues do, after all actual losses through defaults on either interest or principal or both, provide higher net returns over time than higher-grade issues. Therefore, portfolio managers can increase risk-adjusted returns by concentrating on medium-to-lower-grade bonds.

The great secret for success in long-term investing is to avoid serious losses.

Having established a well-diversified portfolio, the bond investor client can then decide whether and how and when to deviate deliberately from the "baseline" portfolio in efforts to increase returns. There are several ways to try:

- Buying or selling individual bonds in anticipation of an improving (or worsening) credit rating

- Switching from one bond market sector priced above its historical averages to another that is priced below its historical averages

- Selling a bond that is temporarily overpriced (perhaps because of a market imperfection) and simultaneously buying a similar bond that is underpriced (a so-called arbitrage swap)

- Changing the average maturity or duration of the entire portfolio by purchasing longer maturities (with call protection) when interest rates are expected to fall and by buying shorter maturities when rates are expected to rise.

However, the evidence that even professional bond managers can consistently and significantly improve results with any of these tactics is feeble. Over long periods of time, gains and losses tend to cancel each other out. How much and whether to invest in bonds at all, not which particular bonds you invest in, will be the most powerful determinant of your overall results.

Even though most investors see their work as active, assertive, and on the offensive, the reality is and should be that stock and bond investing alike are primarily a *defensive* process. The great secret for success in long-term investing is to avoid serious losses. The saddest chapters in the long history of investing are tales about investors who suffered serious losses they brought on themselves by trying too hard or by succumbing to greed.

In deliberate pursuit of wisely determined and explicitly stated objectives of the client, the purpose of the portfolio manager is to control risk and to limit or prevent surprises. The basic responsibility of portfolio managers—since the invention of insurance and pooled risk accounts in merchant shipping on sailing vessels hundreds of years ago—is to control and manage risk.

9

WHY POLICY MATTERS

THE PRINCIPAL REASON you should articulate your long-term investment policy explicitly *and in writing* is to protect your portfolio from ad hoc revisions of sound long-term policy, and to help you adhere to long-term policy when short-term exigencies are most distressing and your policy is most in doubt.

Technology has transformed investing—just as the technology of the Global Position System has transformed navigation. Thanks to technology, investment managers can produce—within the array of feasible results—the intended "relative-to-market" outcome for any particular portfolio. And thanks to the availability of investment technology, investors have every right to achieve results that match their expectations—and their managers' promises. Investment technology is particularly effective over long periods of time.

As a consequence, professional investment management can (and surely should) shift from short-term "conservative caution" and tactical "investment artistry" to a clear focus on explicit long-term investment policies that will achieve specified goals consistently and persistently—through what Disraeli called "constancy to purpose"—within the investor's tolerance for interim market risk.

Bluntly, investors are now free to focus on policy and wise investment counseling and should hold themselves accountable for doing this essential work wisely and well all the time.

History teaches that both investment managers and clients need help if they are to hold successfully to the discipline of long-term commitments. This means restraining themselves from reacting inappropriately to disconcerting short-term data and keeping themselves from taking those unwise actions that seem so "obvious" and urgent to optimists at market highs and to pessimists at market lows. In short, policy is the most powerful antidote to panic. The best shield for long-term policies against the outrageous attacks of acute short-term data and distress are knowledge and understanding—committed to writing.

Policy is the most effective antidote to panic.

The misdemeanors of investment management are almost all due to an inadequate advance understanding by investors of either the *internal* realm of investor objectives or the *external* realm of capital markets and investments, or both. If a major decision is truly fiduciary in nature, it never needs to be done quickly. Time urgent decisions are *never* fiduciary.

All too often, investment policy is both vague and implicit, left to be "resolved" only in haste, when unusually distressing market conditions are putting the pressure on and when it is all too easy to make the wrong decision at the wrong time for the wrong reasons.

Such hasty reviews typically result in selling stocks after they have dropped steeply in value to buy into bonds and other fixed-income investments that will not rise in capital value with the next cycle of the equity market, and vice versa. Clearly, such ill-timed changes in asset mix—selling low and buying high—can be very harmful to the long-term returns of the portfolio.

Comparable harm is also done when recent returns have been higher than should be expected, and investors and their professional advisers shed requisite caution and boldly increase the amount of market risk in the portfolio (buying less seasoned and more volatile stocks). This extra portfolio risk may soon magnify the impact of a subsequent market decline, worsening the ensuing panic and leading another round of "selling low" what investors have previously "bought high."

Investors are people and, like all other people, make decisions based on their emotions when a cool, rational analysis would call for a very different action. Ironically, as human beings, investors like best those upward market movements that are most *adverse* to their long-term interests, and most *dislike* those downward market movements that are, in fact, in their long-term interests.

As much as we may be able to see—in theory—that our long-term interests are best served by lower stock prices, who among us can honestly say we don't feel a warm glow of affection for stocks and markets that have gone up even though it means stocks are now more expensive to buy and future rates of return on our additional investments at these price levels will be lower? Who among us would close our pocketbooks and turn away from the store that puts its most attractive wares on sale at 10, 20, even 30 percent off its recent prices? None of us would say, "I don't want to buy these things when they're on sale; I'll wait until the price goes back up and buy then." But that's exactly how we behave toward investments. When the market drops—putting stocks "on sale"—we stop buying (in fact, we'll even sell in a panic). And when the market rises, we buy more and more enthusiastically. As Jason Zweig puts it, "If we shopped for stocks the way we shop for socks, we'd be better off." But we are wrong when we feel good about stocks having gone up, and we are wrong when we feel bad about stocks having gone down. A falling stock market is the necessary first step to buying low.

"If we shopped for stocks the way we shop for socks, we'd be better off."
—Jason Zweig

This brings us back to the main reason for studying and understanding investments and markets: to protect our portfolios from ourselves. The problem, as Santayana so aptly put it, is that "those who cannot remember the past are condemned to repeat it."

Psychologists studying anxiety and fear have found that four characteristics make people more worried about the perceived riskiness of a situation than the realities would warrant: large-scale consequences; the lack of personal control or influence; unfamiliarity; and sudden occurrence. As a result, we are more fearful of air travel (in which fewer than 30 people are killed and far fewer than 350 hurt in a typical year) than of travel in cars (in which 30,000 people are killed yearly and well over 350,000 injured).

Most investors experience great anxiety over large-scale, sudden, and frightening losses in portfolio value primarily because they have not been well informed in advance that these events are expected and considered normal by those who have studied and understand the long history of stock markets.

Such drops in the market are eminently predictable—not in their timing, but in their magnitude and suddenness. And it is in these periods of anxiety—when the market has been most severely negative—that clients and managers predictably engage in ad hoc "reappraisals" of long-term investment judgment, which allows short-term fears to overwhelm the calm rationality of long-term investment policy.

Investors need protection from their human proclivities toward unrealistic hopes and unnecessary fears—provoked by the emotionally compelling experiences of currently positive or negative surges in the market and by the current opinions that drive them.

The situation is understandable. Investors are not sufficiently informed about the true nature of investment markets and do get surprised. And investment managers are literally inundated by information in written reports; private and group meetings with corporate executives, economists, and analysts; telephone calls; stock price quotations; market transactions that give a compelling urgency to the here and now; and to what others are or may be thinking of doing.

The resulting excessive attention to the present and the immediate future not only produces the "groupthink" errors brilliantly explored by Gustave LeBon in his great book, *The Crowd,* but also distracts attention from careful study of the profound difference between the short-run and the long-run nature of investments.

You can substantially improve your long-term portfolio returns by being sure that you are well informed about the realities of the investment environment in which your portfolio will be managed. You should carefully study the rates of return and patterns of deviation away from the averages over the past several decades, learning as thoroughly as possible why the markets moved as they did. Thoughtful, objective study of the past is the best (and also the least costly!) way to develop an understanding of the basic nature of investments and markets. Markets always have been and always will be surprising, but there is no justification for managers or clients being amazed or shaken by any market development.

Only by understanding the nature of investing and capital markets will you escape the present paradox in which little or no attention is devoted to the truly important work of developing and adhering to wise and appropriate policies that can, over time, achieve realistic and relevant investment objectives and, by preventing mistakes and errors detracting from investment results, achieve superior returns.

10

THE PURPOSE OF POLICY

THE HIGH PURPOSE OF INVESTMENT policy, and of the systematic discovery process prerequisite to it, is to establish useful guidelines for investing that are genuinely appropriate to the realities both of your objectives and the realities of the investments and markets. These are the internal and the external realms of investing, and investment policy must be designed to work well in both realms. In addition, good investment policies are "right" for both the long term and for the many short-term periods that will be experienced in the market. And both clients and managers must hold to them even when they are most uncomfortable.

The value of a set of investment policies depends on the understanding incorporated in them. First come your objectives and tolerance of risk. In institutional investment management, this is the responsibility of the client to develop and of the manager to understand. Individual investors are at least as responsible for clarifying their objectives and making them explicit—best in writing—and then locating the mutual funds that truly match up. Second is the external realm of investments and markets, which is the investment professional's responsibility to understand and explain fully to the investor.

Understanding both dimensions of investment policy and how they can be fit together is a puzzle well worth working out. Investment policy is the explicit linkage between your long-term investment objectives and the daily work of the investment manager. If policy is *not* determined through carefully developed mutual understanding, it *will* be determined in uninformed, anecdotal "ad hocracy." To the extent that you understand the realities of the situation as a whole, you will be able to understand what individual bits of data and specific events mean, and do not mean, for the portfolio you are managing together.

Investment policy is the linkage between your long-term objectives and the daily work of your investment manager.

The usefulness of investment policy depends on the clarity and rigor with which investment objectives, and the policy guidelines established to achieve those objectives, are stated.

The new language derived from modern portfolio theory makes it relatively easy to specify investment objectives and policies and to measure portfolio operations to be sure they are in conformance with agreed-upon policy. This language makes genuine investment counseling possible and should make it feasible for each portfolio manager to achieve excellent performance—not by heroically beating the market, but by faithfully and sensibly carrying out realistic investment policies to achieve each client's objectives.

It is now practical for investment managers and clients to agree objectively on each of these important policy dimensions:

1. The level of market risk to be taken.
2. Whether the level of risk is to be sustained or varied as markets change.
3. Whether individual stock risk or group risk is to be taken or avoided, and the incremental rate of return which such risks, when taken, are expected to produce in the portfolio.

If you wish to select an investment manager who deliberately differentiates his portfolios from the market, then you must take the time to understand clearly *how* he will differentiate his portfolios (by betting heavily on a few stocks, by favoring a particular stock market sector, by investing heavily in cash if he thinks stocks are overpriced?), *when* he will do so (continually, as part of a long-term strategy, or occasionally, as a short-term tactic?), and, most important, *why* he is confident that he will achieve favorable incremental results by taking these actions.

The conceptual simplicity of setting an explicit policy on market risk and agreeing on how the portfolio will be differentiated from a fully diversified market fund is clearly appealing in theory. But it's easier said than done. Because investing is a sampling process, as we will see in more detail in Chapter 11, performance can only be measured in probabilistic terms—in other words, manager X may be likely, but can never be certain, to approximate the market's levels of risk and return. In measuring investment portfolios, we now have good tools, but we do not have precision instruments. There are difficulties with so-called sampling errors, because companies and stocks change in their investment characteristics. (Even as we strive to estimate and adjust for these changes, there will be "noise" in the data that investment managers and their clients are working with.)

There are two major reasons for producing good investment policy guidelines. First in the minds of many is to have a standard by which to monitor professional investment managers. As important as this is, the other reason is paramount: to decide what your own realistic long-term investment goals should be.

Time, as we have seen, is the single most important factor that separates the appropriate investment objective of one portfolio from the appropriate objective of another portfolio. Specifically, it is the length of time over which the portfolio can and will remain committed to a sustained investment policy, and over which you will patiently evaluate investment results versus your objectives and policies.

Liquidity should not be given separate consideration in a well-diversified portfolio *provided* that portfolio is invested in the kind of securities appropriate to its time horizon. For example, even the largest institutional equity portfolio could easily and efficiently be liquidated in a year.

But, of course, if only a year's time were available to the portfolio, it should not be invested in equities at all. It should be in money market instruments to protect your principal against unanticipatable changes in market price. Sufficient liquidity always comes along automatically when investment policy is soundly conceived and implemented.

A puzzling practice, commonly followed in managing pension funds, is maintaining so-called liquidity reserves. The basic reality of the typical pension fund is that it will have a positive cash flow from contributions every year for another generation or more, and so has no need whatever for a liquidity reserve. Of even greater concern, many young 401(k) investors keep much of their portfolios in cash, even though they may be decades away from retirement.

Income requirements are excluded from this discussion of investment policy because the rate of return for an investment portfolio cannot be increased just because you want more money to spend. It is indeed a curious idea that the investment objective for a portfolio should be set according to the funds the investor wants to spend each year. Sometimes this idea shows up in pension funds where the actuarial rate of return assumption will be put forth as a guide to investments. Sometimes it shows up with college presidents insisting on higher endowment fund income to make up for operating deficits. And sometimes it arises when personal funds are asked to finance a more expensive way of life. In all its forms, this practice is nonsense. On the contrary, instead of spending decisions influencing investment decisions, it should be the other way around. Spending decisions should most definitely be governed by the investment results—which follow from investment policies.

Investment policy should be separated from investment operations because they are such different responsibilities. Typically, however, responsibility for both investment policy and operating management of the portfolio are "delegated" to professional investment managers. Mixing together investment policy and portfolio operations—problem definition and problem solving—and delegating *both* to investment managers is not appropriate.

Formulation of long-term investment policy should be clearly and explicitly separated from the operating responsibilities of portfolio management. Only by separating portfolio operations from policy formation can responsibility and accountability be established for each of these two different aspects of investment management.

Portfolio operations should clearly be the responsibility of the investment manager. But setting policy is your job. Of course, they are not kept in isolation from each other. Operating performance will be evaluated objectively against the specified policy intention to be sure operations are in accord with policy. And investment policy will be evaluated objectively against long-term returns in the portfolio to be sure the policies are realistic.

If you have thoughtfully established an investment policy, you have an important advantage. You can evaluate your portfolio managers based on how closely they are adhering to the strategies that will achieve your long-term policy goals. Segregating investment policy (which is your responsibility) from portfolio operations (which are the investment manager's responsibility) is the essential first step in the work of managing the managers. By obliging your investment managers to concentrate entirely on the "how," while you focus on the "what," you prevent their natural preoccupation with present market conditions from corrupting your portfolio's long-term policy. The time horizons of investment managers are typically shorter, often much shorter, than your time horizon as an investor. You should understand this and insist on having *your* time horizons prevail.

Having established investment objectives that are realistic in the market context and appropriate to your time horizon and risk preferences of the investor, you should then specify the investment policies to be followed in pursuit of these stated objectives.

It is by direct comparison with these explicit investment policies—and *only* by comparison with these explicit policies—that the operational performance of the investor or professional investment manager should be measured and evaluated.

For example, it would be both unfair and misleading to attempt an evaluation of the operational performance of a portfolio of growth stocks (or utility stocks or foreign stocks or high-yield stocks) by comparing its results with the overall market averages, because such a mongrelized comparison evaluates a mixture of both policy *and* operations that should be examined separately. Specifically, the performance of a growth stock portfolio should be critiqued in comparison with an index of growth stocks or portfolios of growth stocks. In the same way, a manager of utility stocks should be evaluated only by comparison with the investment opportunities available in utility stocks, just as the manager of a portfolio of Japanese stocks should be evaluated only in comparison with the Japanese market and not with the British, Hong Kong, or American markets.

On the other hand, the *policy* of investing in growth stocks (or utility stocks or Japanese stocks) would be critiqued by examining the superior returns of portfolios of growth stocks (or utility stocks or Japanese stocks) in comparison with other alternative types of stocks and to the market as a whole, over relatively long periods of time.

All too often, a "growth" specialist or a "small cap" specialist will be cheered or jeered—equally unfairly—when her type of specialty is in favor or out of favor in the overall market. And in some cases, the portfolio manager has been credited with "good" performance when, in fact, poor operational performance hindered the attainment of even higher returns that would have resulted from more carefully following an effective policy. A wise old saying goes, "Don't confuse brains with a bull market."

Just as operating performance can be evaluated against policy, policy can be evaluated against performance. If the portfolio manager does not achieve the intended investment result, should the manager be kept and the policy changed? Perhaps the objective is too high. Perhaps the policy is too restrictive for the objective sought. The point is that we can learn from experience if we reflect thoughtfully on what our experience really means.

From time to time, perhaps once every two or three years, a systematic and comprehensive examination of your needs and objectives, market experience, and investment policy is appropriate. While a review of actual results could be moderately useful in critiquing policy, most of the information relevant to a basic examination of investment policy will come not from the specific portfolio, but from more complete—and more relevant— analyses of major sectors of the investment market over very long periods of time.

"Don't confuse brains with a bull market."

In investing, the technology exists to identify a particular portfolio's position relative to the market—just as the Global Position System allows navigators to locate their actual position to within 1 meter anywhere in the world. So investors can have a "cushion for caution" against uncertainty relative to the market—and can sustain long-term commitments to their long-term advantage.

If the policy is found inappropriate, it should be changed and the new policy made explicit. If the operating performance of a professional portfolio manager does not conform with policy, the manager should be replaced, even if his or her deviation from stated policy resulted in a higher rate of return than would have been earned by following stated policy. (Of course, an incompetent portfolio manager would also be replaced, but this is a far easier decision to make.)

A few simple tests of investment policy are these:

1. Is the policy carefully designed to meet your real needs and objectives?

2. Is the policy written so clearly and explicitly that a *competent stranger* could manage the portfolio and conform to your intentions?

3. Would you have been able to sustain commitment to the policies during the capital markets that have actually been experienced over

the past 50 or 60 years—particularly over the past 15 years—when conventional wisdom was most opposed?

4. Would the investor or professional investment manager have been able to maintain fidelity to the policy over the same periods— despite intense daily pressure?

5. Would the policy, if implemented, have achieved your objectives?

Sound investment policies will meet *all* of these tests. Do yours?

11

PERFORMANCE
MEASUREMENT

IF YOU CAN GRASP the following concept, you'll understand all you really need to know about the most important characteristics of the statistics of investment performance.

If many people were in a coin-tossing contest, you could predict two results with great confidence:

1. In the long, *long* run, most coin tossers would average about 50 percent heads and 50 percent tails.

2. In the *short* to intermediate term, however, some of the coin tossers would appear to be somewhat better than average at tossing heads—and a very few would *appear* to be very much better than average at tossing heads.

If we were to inspect the record, surely the data on each individual coin tosser would be clear and objective, but we'd know better than to think the *past* results would be good predictors of *future* results in coin tossing. Sooner or later, each of the coin tossers would become more and more *average*. Statisticians call this powerful yet common phenomenon *regression to the mean*.

Performance measurement is least useful when needed most—and is needed least when it could be most effective.[1] This chapter explains why.

As a professional investment manager is given more and more discretion to deviate from a market fund and to take more and more risks of different kinds—market risk, group risk, and individual stock risk—the difficulty of determining how much of any specific period's portfolio return is due to skill or chance increases rapidly.

Performance data that are sufficiently timely to have relevance for practical decisions on how well a manager is really doing, and whether a manager should be changed, are based on too small a sample or too short a time period to provide enough information to make an accurate decision. And results for longer time periods—which offer greater accuracy—will not be sufficiently timely to be relevant for current decisions on how well managers are doing, unless the results are overwhelmingly good or bad.

Measurements of a portfolio investment performance do not, at least in the short run, "mean what they say." Performance measurement services do not report "results." They report statistics. These statistics are arbitrary samples drawn period by period from a most unusual and continuous process—the process of managing complex, changing portfolios of securities in the context of a large, dynamic, always changing, and often turbulent free and competitive capital market. The stocks and bonds in the portfolios are frequently changed; companies and their businesses are always changing in many different ways; and the factors that most affect the prices of securities (fear, greed, inflation, politics, economic news, business profits, investors' expectations, and so forth) never cease to change.

So long as the portfolio is not being cashed in, this multidimensional set of change forces will go on and on revising the value of the portfolio. There are no real "results" until the process stops and the portfolio is finally liquidated. Regression to the mean is a central reality in the pattern so frequently observed in long data time series (like investment management and coin tossing). And the manager whose favorable investment performance in the recent past *appears* to be proving he or she is the better manager is often—not always, but all too often—about to produce *below-average* results. Why? Usually, a large part of the apparently "superior" performance was *not* due to superior skill that will continue to produce superior results, but was instead due to that particular manager's sector of

[1]Professor Barr Rosenberg estimates it would require 70 years of observations to show conclusively that even 200 basis points of incremental annual return resulted from superior investment management *skill* rather than chance.

the market enjoying above-average rates of return—or luck. However, when the tide turns, the behavior of that segment of the market that propelled the manager ahead will hold him or her back. That's part of why investment managers' results so often regress to the mean. Another reason is this: With so many professional managers so very good at what they do, it is difficult to beat the crowd because the crowd is full of *professionals* who work very hard and are always striving to learn how to be better. And, as a whole, these professionals play the game very, very well.

Long-term performance data will also have a survivor bias and a new-firm bias. Here's why. New investment management firms are launched by managers who can show off the superior results they have achieved in recent years—often with a previous employer. Firms that continue to get good results typically take on more new accounts, while older firms that *appear* to have poor performance may lose accounts. Those with the worst results will go out of business. (As in any field, the doctors bury their mistakes.) So the average manager in business today will have slightly better performance than the average manager who was in business 25 or 50 years ago. And advertising will be touting the managers with the "best records," so investors will hear most often from those who've been most successful—so far.

Statisticians debate among themselves whether it takes 40, 60, or 80 years to determine definitively whether the incremental return obtained by a particular portfolio is attributable to luck or to skill. Of course, the debate is academic because almost no investment manager has reliable performance data going back 40 or 60 years. Moreover, by the time performance data is good enough for investors to act on the conclusion, the optimal time for action will be long past.

Since each investment manager's actual performance will—like the market's return—be drawn from a bell-shaped probability distribution around a mean or average annual rate of return, investment objectives and performance measurements should be understood and specified in terms of both the mean or average rate of return and a distribution around that mean.

Recognizing that measurements of performance are statistics leads to an appreciation that, as with any series of statistics, each data point must be read not as an exact number but only as an *approximation* of an exact number.

For users of performance measurement, the big problem is separating three very different factors that are mixed into the overall performance data. One factor is the "sampling error," or the probability that the statistics do not precisely equal the facts. As in any sample, there will be imprecision or uncertainty. In investment performance data, the sampling error is the degree to which the particular portfolio, for the particular time period, is a good or a biased sample of the manager's work.

The second factor is that during the measurement period, the market conditions may have been a favorable or unfavorable environment for the particular manager's way of investing. For example, investors in small-capitalization stocks have had very favorable and quite unfavorable market environments during the past decades. As a result, they have all looked better than they really were in some years, and looked worse than they really were in other periods. This is why most investment managers should be measured over at least one full cycle of up markets and down markets.

The third factor is the skill—or *lack* of skill—of the investment manager. This is what many clients and managers most want to measure. But here's the rub: In the very short run, sampling errors will have a much larger impact on the measured results than will the manager's skill.

To be specific, it would not be at all unusual for an investment manager's results to be in a range that was within 2 percent of the return that would be expected most of the time from a broadly diversified portfolio with the same level of market risk. As noted earlier, it would take many years of performance measurement to know whether the *apparently* superior results were due to the manager's skill or just to good luck. By the time you had gathered enough data to determine whether your manager really was skillful or just lucky, at least one of you would probably have died of old age.

The power of regression to the mean in investing is illuminated in Figure 11-1. Each column shows—for each quintile—the average annual compound returns achieved by investing with *last* year's median manager for the *next* year. The final column shows the 10-year cumulative average. Even a brief inspection of the annual columns—and particularly the 10-year final column—shows that *past performance does not predict future performance.*

It would take many years of measurement to determine if a portfolio manager's "superior" results were due to skill or luck.

Take a careful look at the data: As you'll soon see, there's nothing to see. *There is no pattern.* Like Sherlock Holmes's dog that didn't bark, this

FIGURE 11-1   Subsequent year median annual returns for managers, sorted by past year's returns

Source: Cambridge Associates.

Quintile Performance	1985	1986	1987	1988	1989	1990	1991	1992	1993	1994	10-Year Average
First	19.8	4.7	16.0	25.3	−0.2	39.6	8.5	17.4	−0.1	33.0	15.7
Second	19.7	5.3	16.4	25.8	−1.6	34.3	9.6	15.1	0.0	35.1	15.3
Third	18.5	4.4	16.7	28.8	−3.4	32.2	9.5	13.1	0.4	34.2	14.8
Fourth	17.3	4.8	18.7	30.3	−2.1	30.9	10.3	11.2	0.3	33.9	14.9
Fifth	16.6	6.2	20.8	33.1	−6.1	34.0	10.1	10.9	1.1	31.7	15.1

lack of pattern *is* the pattern. As Dorothy Parker once said in dismissing the possibility of visiting a particular city: "There's no *there* there."

With most of the buying and selling in the stock and bond markets now being done by professionals, the pricing mechanism is what statisticians would describe as open and fair. (Rough, perhaps very rough—particularly on amateurs—but statistically fair all the same.)

So, over very long periods, the median or average return obtained by most professional investors would be expected to be close to the market average (such as the S&P 500 Index)—*minus* at least 1 percent of operating costs each year for advisory fees and commissions on transactions and custody expenses. The professionals would be expected to lag *behind* the market (as explained in Chapter 1). And this is what studies of investment performance consistently show. The average professionally managed fund has a rate of return equal to the market *minus* the costs to participate in the market.

A major problem for the investment managers and for their clients is the considerable dispersion in performance being produced by the same investment managers when managing portfolios with the same investment policies. Results should be the same, but the differences are substantial. For the investment manager, such dispersion is clearly an important problem in quality control.

For you, a key problem will be in deciding how to interpret the results. Should you accept the manager's assurances that below-average results will surely be reversed in the coming period and that you should stay? Or should you reject the assurance, assert that the manager is "out of control," and terminate the relationship?

One thing is certain: You should insist on full disclosure of the performance of *all* the manager's portfolios so you can get a good sample of the manager's overall achievement. You should not try to infer a professional manager's overall performance from your own portfolio—a sample of one!

Information is data with a purpose. Because performance measurement can only be useful when a valid standard has been clearly established, performance measurement depends on a clear and explicit investment policy. And the purpose of regular measurements of portfolio performance must be to determine whether current portfolio *operations* are in faithful accord with long-term *policy*.

Performance measurement cannot and will not be useful in measuring results. Only an approximate answer can be given to a question like "What rate of return was earned in this quarter?" and that approximation will not be useful unless results are extreme. However, quite useful information can be drawn from performance measurement on the investment *process*. If portfolio operations have not been in accord with agreed policy and the investment manager's agreed-upon mission, it is not really important whether current portfolio results happen to be above (lucky you) or below (unlucky you) the results that would be expected had policy been followed faithfully. In either case, the truly important information is that the portfolio and the portfolio manager are out of control. Sooner or later, this lack of control will show up in losses—uncontrolled and unrecoverable losses.

The impossibility of using short- or even intermediate-term performance measurement to manage managers by acting on "results" is what makes it so essential that clients and investment managers establish and sustain wise long-term investment policies.

There are other practical problems with performance measurement, particularly when it is used to measure whether a portfolio is or is not "within policy."

First, estimates of the risk of individual stocks and the risks of groups of stocks are estimates of probable *future* price behavior based on the best available estimates of *past* behavior. While past patterns are usually our best available guide to likely future patterns, the future is sure to differ in significant measure from the past.

Second, the relationship between the "market" and a specific stock or portfolio of stocks is not constant. The relationship "drifts." Consequently, the past will not be a perfectly reliable basis upon which to estimate the current or the future behavior of a stock or group of stocks.

Third, the amount of "drift" in the relationship over time will be less for stocks of major companies in established industries and will be more for stocks in small or marginally successful companies, particularly in rapidly changing industries.

Fourth, even the most rigorous statistical descriptions of individual stocks or groups of stocks are themselves estimates and are stated in terms of statistical probabilities, with the implicit understanding that there will be a distribution of actual experience around the expected mean.

Fifth, just one or two decisions—perhaps brilliantly skillful, perhaps lucky, perhaps both—can make a powerful difference to the reported performance of a portfolio.[2] Professional investment managers will recognize how often one of their portfolios has enjoyed far better results than another portfolio simply because, when implementing a strategic decision to invest heavily in an industry group, the stock used in one portfolio did very well while the stock used in another portfolio did badly.

Sixth and most important is the problem of "end period dominance." Almost always, the most important factor in the reported performance of an investor or a professional investment manager is not his or her skill but the choice of starting date and ending date. Many of the most impressive "gee whiz" charts of investment performance become quite ordinary by simply adding or subtracting one year at the start or the end of the period shown.

More and more investors (and professional investment managers) are quite properly dissatisfied with the convention of comparing the results of their portfolio to the results of a group of other portfolios of similar size, even though these portfolios do not necessarily have the same long-term investment policies. A portfolio's operations should only be judged in comparison with its policy commitment and the results that should reasonably be expected given that policy.

At the very least, results for one portfolio should be compared only to funds with a similar prescribed level of market risk. And one of the key criteria on which performance should be measured is this: Did the portfolio manager keep the portfolio's market risk at the level specified in the statement of investment policy?

In addition, it would be more equitable and more informative to compare a portfolio's results with other portfolios with a similar mission: growth stock portfolios versus growth stock portfolios; conservative stock

---

[2]The classic example was the impact of a spectacularly successful, but almost accidentally made, investment in Digital Equipment. With it, American Research and Development (AR&D, a venture capital fund) significantly outperformed the market averages. Without it, AR&D would have underperformed the market during its 20-year life.

portfolios versus conservative stock portfolios; "small-cap" stock portfolios to "small-cap" stock portfolios, and so on.

In the same vein, the performance of an equity portfolio should be based on the total assets available for equity investment, not just the portion that happened to be in stocks—with cash positions excluded. The same applies to bond portfolios: Cash reserves should be counted in, not counted out. (Whether the use of cash reserves helped or hurt performance compared with a fully invested portfolio can and should be examined separately.)

For balanced accounts, the equity portfolio (cash reserves included) should be measured in comparison to similar equity funds, and the bond portfolio (cash reserves included) should be compared to similar bond funds, and the impact of shifts in the stock/bond mix should be reported and examined separately to see if these shifts in asset mix are contributing to overall results.

One of the great frustrations thoughtful investment professionals have had with typical performance measurement is that bad decisions with favorable outcomes are often well received by innocent clients while good decisions with temporarily unfavorable outcomes can lead to the loss of an account. Variance from expected and intended results are just as "wrong" when the apparent result is *above* expectation as when the result is *below* expectation. (A ship is just as far off course when 10 miles *west* of its objective as when it is 10 miles *east* of its objective.) Sure it's nice for the investor to get a higher return than a lower return, but either one is "off target," and the investor should not confuse good luck (or bad luck) with the manager's skill.

Portfolios should be compared with portfolios with a similar mission, such as growth versus growth or small cap versus small cap.

More serious—because it is more common—is the pattern of clients choosing managers just after they have had "their kind of market," and imputing to these managers a special set of skills and genius that will be impossible to sustain after that market environment changes.

For example, a "growth" manager may outperform other growth managers only to have some clients terminate because results were below the returns earned over the same time by "value" managers when the prices of value stocks were doing particularly well.

The final problem with performance measurement is its perverse tendency to stimulate counterproductive thinking and behavior by diverting your interest and attention to short-term operating results and away from long-term policy. The process of measuring almost certainly influences the phenomenon being measured, as the physicist Heisenberg elucidated years ago with his "Principle of Indeterminacy." As usually reported in their two-decimal form for a known time period, investment returns sound almost microscopically accurate: "Over the 12 months ending June 30, manager A returned 27.53 percent." That apparent precision gives such performance numbers a legitimacy they do not deserve, since they are in truth a sampling, not a measurement, of investment returns. (To be truly accurate, the statement should be revised to read: "A tiny minority of this manager's clients—those who opened their accounts last July 1, liquidated their accounts this June 30 and neither added nor subtracted any money at any other time—earned 27.53 percent. All the manager's other clients either earned more or less than that; in some cases much more or much less. Furthermore, the manager's performance over this period tells next to nothing about his future performance.")

By expressing recent short-term returns in such precise terms, performance measurement turns our heads: It makes us believe that the short term is meaningful and that the long term will resemble it. There is a strong human tendency to think about the phenomenon being measured in the time interval used in the measuring and to let the measurement interval dominate the time horizon that actually should be used. Short-term thinking is the enemy of long-term investment success.

Since the way performance is measured often determines the investment manager's compensation—and, so even, his entire approach to the market—you should be sure that you and your portfolio managers are measuring the right things.

A form of Gresham's law ("bad money drives out good") can easily take over, as portfolio managers and investors alike allow the obsession with short-term performance to drive out the thoughtful concern with longer-term policy objectives. (Quarterly performance, as we've just discussed, really can't be "measured." The sample is too small to give useful information.) This can easily lead to a series of constant adjustments to

long-term policy in an effort to improve short-term performance—with
portfolio risk levels being reduced after a period of poor returns (when risk
should, if anything, be raised) and being increased after a period of good
returns (when risk should be lowered or at least kept constant). Both are
clearly counterproductive. The tail (short-term performance) should not be
allowed to wag the dog (long-term policy).

If the risk level is to be changed, it would make more sense to change it
in the opposite direction, reducing risk after recently favorable results and
increasing risk after recently adverse results. Taking this counterintuitive
action is, of course, very difficult to do—for both investors and professional investment managers.

The main reason for measuring performance is to improve investor-
manager communication. The purpose of performance measurement is not
to provide answers, but rather to identify questions that investors and managers should explore together to be sure they have a good mutual understanding of what is contributing to and what is detracting from investment
performance. Ask the child's favorite series of questions: Why? Why? Why?

Central to good investor-manager communication is information that
shows whether the portfolio is being managed in accordance with agreed-
upon policy, particularly policy on market risk and on the type of investments in which the manager is expected to specialize. The impact of these
two policy parameters should be measured and reported on a regular basis.
The better mutual funds do.

The most effective and informative use of investment performance data
is to determine not whether a manager's portfolio performance is superior
or inferior, but whether a manager is conforming to his or her promised and
expected mission. A *value* stock manager should be producing good results
relative to value stocks; a *growth* manager should be producing good
results relative to growth stocks.

The key concept is this: *Any unexpected and unexplained deviation
from realistic expectation is poor performance.* (A sensible proxy for "realistic expectations" of a mutual fund is the average performance of other
funds with similar investment objectives.) A *large* unexplained deviation is
very poor performance. And as every user of statistical techniques of quality control[3] will know, it makes *no difference* whether the deviation is *above*
or *below* expectation. Sure, we investors are trained to think higher returns

---

[3]Deming and Juran built great careers helping manufacturers achieve superior product quality through such statistical techniques for analyzing consistency and conformance to plan
and intention.

are better returns. And in the long run, they certainly are. But in the shorter run, deviating above *or* below expectation indicates the manager is out of conformance to his or her mission. And out of conformance usually means out of control[4]—with unhappy results the very probable eventual outcome.

The final area of "performance measurement" is clearly qualitative. Does the manager's explanation of his or her decisions make good sense? Is the manager doing as promised—making the kinds of decisions that were "advertised"? Are the manager's actions consistent with his or her words at the previous meeting? When the manager changes the portfolio's structure, do the explanations make good common sense? As a thoughtful, interested client, do you find your confidence in the manager's abilities, knowledge, and judgment rising as you have more and more discussions—or is it falling?

Investors should give real weight to these "soft" qualitative factors because over and over again, this is where the best signals of real trouble first surface—long before the problem is evident in the "hard" qualitative data.

Even more important, sophisticated investors have been able to stay with professional managers that made good qualitative sense even when the quantitative measures of performance were disappointing because the manager happened to be temporarily out of tune with the market. In many cases, subsequent performance has been very rewarding to both manager and client. In fact, a good test of the care with which a client has chosen a manager would be this: If the manager underperformed the market because his or her particular style was out of favor, albeit skillfully implemented, the client would cheerfully assign substantially *more* funds to the manager in question because the client would recognize that the manager will outperform the overall market averages when investment fashion favors his or her style. This is the favorable side of regression to the mean—so why not take advantage of it?

---

[4]Investors might think of performance in driving. Even if you plan to turn right a mile farther on, swerving off the road to the right is just as badly out of control as swerving off the road to the left. It's the same with investment performance.

12

MANAGING
MANAGERS

VERY FEW INVESTMENT MANAGERS and very few investor clients
are well satisfied with their present relationships. And it's their
own fault. Too little attention is devoted by either clients or
managers to designing and developing truly successful relationships. While investment managers can readily be faulted for
not taking more initiative in this area, the primary responsibility does and
always will rest with the clients.

Great clients make great firms, and clients of investment managers can
do real service for their managers by combining three attributes: rigorous
insistence on adherence to the explicitly agreed-upon mission; candor in
discussing areas of dissatisfaction or uncertainty; and patience with the
understandably human nature of investment managers—encouraging the
glum and disappointed, cautioning the euphoric and self-assured.

Clients should assert themselves in developing good working relationships with investment managers for several reasons. First, as discussed in
Chapter 1, clients know (or certainly ought to know) what is unusual and
important about their investment objectives. And it is the client's responsibility to project this knowledge into the process of formulating long-term
objectives and investment policy.

Second, investment managers are so deeply immersed in the demand-
ing details of daily investment operations that it is implausible that they

would—alone and unaided—find time and interest to think through the specific circumstances of each client and develop sensitively separate policies for each.

Third, the real need in most investment relationships is not for more *investment* management, but for more *management* management, and this set of skills is far more likely to be found among corporate executives, foundation trustees, and makers of trusts with general management experience and orientation than among investment management specialists.

Finally, it is the client who has the most to gain from developing successful and purposeful relationships. While the manager can lose the account, his downside risk is the loss of a fee; the client's downside risk is no less than the health of his whole portfolio.

How many different investment managers should an investor use? Using mutual funds, an investor can usually find several different *styles* or concepts of investing offered by one major family of funds. All of the funds offered by a family will be organizationally accountable for the same standards of professionalism, reasonable fees, and investor services. That's why it makes sense to concentrate on one or two fund families whose long-term investment results and business values and practices you respect.[1]

Here are some suggestions on how to be a good client. First, start by knowing yourself and your organization and what your investment objectives and staying power really are. You should examine your capacity to tolerate investment adversity needs examination in different time frames. For example, it's one thing to know your ability to handle what might be called quarter-to-quarter fluctuations. They are relatively modest and soon reversed. It's another to absorb and accept a full bear market, particularly one that lasts longer and plummets more than normal; for example, ask how you would feel if stocks lost more than 37 percent of their value, as they did in 1973–74, shrinking $1,000 to less than $630 in two awful years.

The perspective within which to test yourself is not from the calm armchair of the market historian who can see "how it all worked out" in the end. Instead, you'll want to think very carefully about the way you would feel and might react to the dreadful experience of a severe bear market at its worst moment, when the next stage is not known and may be even worse!

---

[1]If in doubt, ask your employer's pension executive or your accountant for the names of a few organizations they would respect most for *very* long-term investment, write for the literature on *all* their funds and on their organization, study this information carefully, and then make your own final selection. Discipline your decision making with the determination to stay invested for the very long term.

This kind of candid self-critique will help you determine your true investment staying power.

Determining your tolerance for pain and your investment staying power will provide you with the basis upon which you can set the level of market risk that you can and will live with. Don't overcommit. Know your internal realities, and stay within your own limitations. As my father, Raymond W. Ellis advised: "Never risk more than you know you can afford to lose."

"Never risk more than you know you can afford to lose."

Second, learn to understand the *external* realities of the investment markets and do not expect more of your managers than they will be able to deliver. If you insist on "beat the market" performance, you *will* find managers who will make the promise. But can they keep it?

Third, select managers who are clearly competent to complete the mission you have in mind for them, who understand the mission and accept it, and with whom you would genuinely enjoy working.

Finally, strive always to discipline yourself to keep faith with your own commitment to a steady, long-term program. Try to follow the advice of Caesar: *De minimus non curat praetor!* (Don't be concerned with small matters!)

The main features of mutually advantageous manager-client relationships are not difficult to describe. First, the relationship should be designed and intended to last a long time. Changing managers is costly and disruptive for both manager and client, and usually comes only after an unhappy series of misunderstandings and mistakes leads to endemic mistrust.

As in any good business relationship, the responsibilities and undertakings of each party should be both realistic and clear. In particular, the investment manager's "mission" should be both explicit and in writing, and mutually agreed upon. It should be within the competence of the investment manager; it should be realistic and reasonable relative to the market; and it should be sufficient to satisfy your legitimate and informed expectations. If these three criteria are *not* being met, the client should get together with the investment manager until they have agreed on a mission statement that does meet all three tests.

Second, the relationship will usually be centered on quarterly or semi-annual meetings, organized to achieve the success in working together desired by both investment manager and client. Before each meeting, an agenda should be prepared by the client and all relevant documentation should be provided, usually by the manager, with ample time for careful preparation by both manager and client. (The emphasis on *relevant* documentation is deliberate: It takes little genius to flood a meeting with sufficient trivia to camouflage the central issues.)

The investment manager's "mission" should be both explicit and in writing, and mutually agreed upon.

Each meeting should begin with a careful review of the investment manager's mission—the agreed-upon investment policies of the portfolio through which the manager is expected to accomplish the mutually intended long-term objective—to see if any modification in either objective or policy is appropriate. If they have no changes in mission to propose, both client and investment manager should explicitly reaffirm the mission statement. If either client or manager wishes to propose a change, the proposal and the rationale supporting it should be prepared in advance and distributed as one of the meeting preparation documents so all participants can study and think through the proposed change. There should, of course, be no surprises in this most important part of the meeting.

Discussion of specific portfolio operations—purchases and sales of specific securities—should be on an exception basis and should be brief. This portion of the meeting should *not* be "interesting." Clients should not accept colorful recitations of war stories or capsule reviews of specific stocks: They are fun, but they are only entertainment. Instead, this part of the meeting should be a straightforward confirmation that the manager has sensibly and faithfully followed agreed-upon policy. Like a successful medical examination, the review of operations should be thorough, expeditious, and conclude with the assurance, "as expected, everything is fine."

At most, the review of operations and reaffirmation of the investment manager's mission should take just 10 minutes. The balance of the meeting time, usually another half hour, can best be devoted to a thoughtful and detailed discussion of almost any one topic of importance to both the client and the manager.

At least once each year, the main topic should be a candid review—led by the client—of the client's overall financial situation and the context into which the investment portfolio fits.

Similarly, for institutional investors it will usually be relevant for the investment manager to devote one meeting to a discussion of his organization's professional and business development—with particular emphasis on the investment management firm's long-term business and professional policies and commitments—and the importance to his firm of the kind of account represented by the client. For individual investors, a written description of the manager's desired clientele and the service for which the manager intends to be accountable can be useful.

Other meetings can constructively be devoted to discussions of a major economic development, a major portfolio commitment, or discussion of the changing economics or investment attraction of a particular industry. The important purpose of these topical discussions is to enable the client to take a deep look into the thinking process of the investment managers.

Meetings should *not* be used as they almost always are: for a brief Cook's tour of the investment world that might include superficial comments on the economic outlook, recent changes in interest rates, a review of minor changes in the weightings of industry groups in the equity portfolio, a quick recap of modest shifts in quality ratings in the bond portfolio, and concluding with some interesting insights into specific decisions.

Such discussions can easily deteriorate into a superficial "show and tell" report of current events. Without really digging into any of the major decisions made, they can use up the time that might otherwise be devoted to serious discussions of subjects of potentially enduring importance to a successful relationship—and to the portfolio.

A written summary (of perhaps three to five pages) should be prepared and distributed after each meeting and kept for future reference. One good suggestion would be to have alternating meetings summarized by the clients and investment managers.

Meetings should not be used to bring new members of the client's investment committee up-to-date. Such catch-up briefings should be conducted separately, perhaps earlier on the same day as the main meeting. With a good written record of each prior meeting, these catch-up briefings can be accomplished both quickly and reliably—to everyone's benefit.

Three functions can be served by an investment committee, and experience suggests they can be served best when carefully *separated.* The three functions are:

1. Determining *investment policy* for the whole fund over the very long term—focusing on long-term asset mix, riskiness, and so forth, and making careful, documented, and explicit judgments about what's "right" for the particular fund and feasible for long-term investment in the capital markets.

2. Dividing the total portfolio's overall investment policy into specific assignments for specific investment managers so each will have agreed-upon defined benchmarks or "normal" portfolios—with agreed-upon expectations for investment results in various market scenarios.

3. Evaluating the period-to-period effectiveness with which each investment manager is performing in meeting that manager's specific assignment.

The meeting's agenda for decisions to be made would match *each* of these three functions:

1. Is the asset mix "right" for this particular fund *and* feasible over the very long term? (Or to put it the other way around, is there a compelling near-term reason to change the previously "right" long-term policy to a *new* "right" long-term policy?)

    Since changes in a pension plan's or an endowment's needs or even in a typical individual's situation—*or* changes in the basic nature of the capital markets—will usually develop only gradually, decisions to change investment policy seldom will be made. They *might* be given careful review once a year; they should be reviewed carefully after any *major* change in the needs of the investor.

2. Given the overall investment policy—after making any sound, long-term adjustment—would it make sense to make any changes in the assignments given specific managers? Again, change is unlikely and should be infrequent.

3. Given their performance relative to agreed-upon benchmarks *or* changes in the committee's assessment of each manager's capabilities to perform its mission, are any changes in managers called for?

Again, if the client has done thorough and rigorous thinking through all of the relevant issues, such changes are unlikely to be made. And experience shows that the best decision would be the "counterintuitive" decision: Assign *more* money to the manager who has been recently "*under*performing"—because the well-chosen manager will probably be "underperforming" only because his or her style is temporarily out of favor—and will likely *out*perform when market conditions are more favorable to his or her style.

After formulating and implementing a sound investment policy, changes should be made carefully and infrequently.

If this three-tier approach were taken, the reports from consultants or staff to the investment committee would match these tiers, but in *reverse* order:

- Should any managers be changed? The normal expectation would be "No." If any manager is identified as "up for review," the staff or consultant would provide a rigorous review of the cases for and against action. (Note that "bad performance" is *any* substantial deviation from expectation, whether above or below.) If none are identified, discussion would be concentrated on . . .

- Should the amounts assigned to specific managers be changed? (For example, shifting assets *from* managers who have had quite favorable environments for their type of investing *to* managers whose style of investing has been "difficult.") If such actions *are* proposed (which they should be as seldom as possible), staff or consultants would provide the cases for and against each specific action. If none are proposed, discussion would concentrate on . . .

- Should the long-term policy on asset mix be changed? If not, would a significant "temporary" deviation be appropriate? If not, the work of the committee is over and the formal part of the meeting is completed.

In this format, decisions are on an "exception" basis and decisions to act are few and far between *because* the investment committee has "done its homework" rigorously and thus decided on long-term policy *and* on determination of specific missions for managers *and* on specific managers (and so would make few, if any, changes on any of these fronts).

How long would an ideal meeting on action decisions take? About five minutes—with *no* actions taken because none were needed. As every experienced manager of continuous-process factories knows, one indication of a well-run plant is that "nothing interesting is going on," because anything "interesting" is a *problem* and a well-run plant is problem-free. It does not need corrections.

The most important contribution clients can make to a successful relationship with an investment manager is to select the right manager to begin with. Of course, the first step in selecting the right manager is to know what investment mission the chosen manager will be expected to fulfill.

Prospective investment managers should be examined in three major areas: professional investment competence; commitment to client service; and soundness of business strategy. Of the three areas, professional investment competence is quite properly given the greatest attention.

A prospective investment management firm should have a clear concept of how it will add value to managing the client's portfolio. Such a concept can be based on the manager's perception of an opportunity—or a problem—in the market that presents favorable opportunities for this particular firm to increase the portfolio's rate of return.

In addition to a cogent concept of how to add value, the investment manager should have developed a sensible process for making decisions to *implement* that concept and should have a valid record of achievement of the results intended by his process to fulfill his concept.

Keep notes on the answers your investment manager gives to your questions. They can be brief but must be saved for future use—in comparing the answers you get at other times to the same or similar questions. This simple technique has been used for years—perhaps even for centuries—by the managers of the Scottish trusts.

The concept of using multiple managers has become increasingly popular among large clients in recent years. Several reasons are given:

1. The client can select specialist managers skilled in each of several different kinds of investing wanted.

2. The client can diversify against the risk of one manager's investment concept being out of tune with the overall market (as will surely happen from time to time).

3. Managers who fail to perform can be terminated more easily when they manage only part of the client's funds.

The problem with multiple managers is that the positive reasons become increasingly ephemeral as the number of managers increases. While it may be feasible to select one or two superior managers in a particular specialty, it's harder and harder to pick three or five or seven. There just aren't that many truly superior managers around.

While diversification does increase with each additional manager, when the separately managed portfolios are amalgamated into one fund and analyzed, it becomes clear that each additional manager adds less and less incremental diversification, but does incur higher and higher operating costs and fees—and moves closer and closer to the investment characteristics of the market index.

Since index funds are readily available at low cost, the use of more and more different managers cannot be to reduce risk, because that can be accomplished more easily and more cheaply with a market fund.

Rationally, if the client is prepared to pay the higher fees inherent in multiple management, the objective must be to increase returns by finding managers who can find and exploit the occasional but significant opportunities that might arise from mispricing errors of other managers.

Realistically, important opportunities of this kind are only infrequently found. Therefore, the client might well force the manager to place all his bets on a very small number of decisions he believes are most attractive. If this forcing is not done, the client with multiple managers will most certainly be overpaying for excess diversification. Individual investors who do not wish to place all their assets in index funds might do well, then, to place their remaining assets in funds run by active managers who focus their holdings in relatively few stocks.

The argument that managers can be more easily terminated—with less harm to the fund and less harm to the management firm—if the account is relatively small to both parties is, of course, true. But it may be pernicious. Clients might understandably be less careful in selecting or supervising managers they know they can terminate. And managers may be too cautious in asserting their best investment judgment if these clients might, during an interim period of adverse "performance," terminate them. Most investment managers believe, rightly or wrongly, that the tolerance of their clients for performance that differs significantly from the market and for portfolio decisions that differ from the conventional is least when needed most.

Consequently, unless guided by clearly defined investment objectives and policies, investment managers may be tempted to act as though their real goal is not to maximize investment results for their clients, but to maximize their probability of keeping the account. This could and does result in most portfolios being stuck in the "muddle of the middle," producing a high-cost but imperfect market portfolio.[2]

---

[2]Indeed, roughly 85 percent of the returns of the typical large-stock mutual fund can be explained simply by the movements of the Standard & Poor's 500 stock market average.

Good clients will, if they decide to use active managers, insist that their managers adhere to the discipline of following through on agreed-upon investment policy. In other words, the investor client will be equally justified and reasonable to terminate a manager for out-of-control results *above* the market as for out-of-control results *below* the market. Staying with a manager who is not conforming his or her portfolio performance or to prior promises is *speculation*—and ultimately will be "punished."

But staying with the competent investment manager who is conforming to his or her own promises—*particularly* when out of phase with the current market environment—shows real "client prudence" in investing and ultimately will be well rewarded.[3]

Rare is the manager who achieves long-term results that are substantially superior after adjustment for riskiness. That's why investors will find it distressingly difficult to find managers who can and will achieve consistently superior results. And that's why experience teaches that reaching for "the best" manager so frequently produces real disappointment for investors. Like Icarus, trying too hard can lead to serious harm. Switching around among mutual funds is what causes the average mutual fund investor to obtain long-term returns that produce a distressing *one-third less* than the average mutual fund. This serious slippage is the self-inflicted pain caused by those who do not or cannot appreciate the importance of fidelity.

Professional pension executives responsible for pension funds—often advised by experienced consultants with massive databases and numerous staff researchers who diligently and constantly monitor managers—have this set of experiences: The managers they *hire* tend to underperform the managers they *fired* and replaced. So take extra time and care to select the manager you would be ready to "double up" with whenever recent performance is below the market averages.

---

[3]As I know from experience. In the mid-1970s, I increased my commitment to John Neff's Gemini Fund—a lot. The following 20 years (thanks to John's great work as "the professional investor's favorite investment professional") were very well rewarded—with minimal risk.

13

HOW TO LOSE

I NVESTORS MUST LIVE WITH losses and losing. The challenge—and the opportunity—is to lose less and to accept short-term losses as a necessary reality along the pathway to long-term gains. In other words, only lose "on purpose"—as a means to a desirable end.

One way to increase success in lifelong investing is to reduce and remove errors. (Ask any golfer or tennis player!) Here's a list of mistakes investors make:

- Trying too hard—striving to get more from your investments or from your investment managers than they can produce repetitively and reliably over the long term. Being too aggressive can be and usually is expensive. In a recent paper entitled "Why *Do* Investors Trade Too Much?," Terrance Odean, finance professor at the University of California at Davis, looked at nearly 100,000 stock trades made by retail investors at a major discount brokerage firm from 1987 through 1993. He found, on average, that the stocks these investors bought underperformed the market by 2.7 percentage points over the following year, while the stocks they sold outperformed the market by 0.5 points in the following year.[1] Similarly, in a paper published by Brookings Institution, economists Josef Lakonishok, Andrei Shleifer, and Robert Vishny showed that the stock trades made by pension fund managers subtracted 0.78 percent from the returns they would

[1]This paper is available on the internet at: *http://gsm.ucdavis.edu/~odean.*

have earned by keeping their portfolios constant.[2] Finally, the Plexus Group, a consulting firm that researches the costs of trading for professional money managers, studied more than 80,000 trades by 19 investment firms and found that the typical purchase of a stock added 0.67 percent to a fund's short-term return—but that the typical sales subtracted 1.08 percent.[3]

No wonder Philp Carret, the 100-year old founder of the Pioneer Fund, has said, "Turnover usually indicates a failure of judgment. It's extremely difficult to figure out when to sell anything."

- Not trying hard enough—usually by being cautious for short-term reasons when successful investing requires long-term thinking and long-term behavior. Being too defensive can be expensive. For example, during the past two decades it has been costly to hold even a moderate cash reserve within an equity portfolio or to concentrate bond investments on governments (instead of on GNMA pass-throughs).

- Making *investment* decisions just for *tax* reasons.

- Attempting market timing.

- Allowing short-term concerns to dominate long-term commitments.

Short-term losses are an unavoidable cost of long-term investment success.

- Not composing—and writing down—your program of saving and spending.

- Not composing—and writing down—your investment objectives and your investment policy or program.

- Procrastinating on estate planning.

- Not taking advantage of *time* when making decisions about gifts and bequests.

[2]"The Structure and Performance of the Money Management Industry," Brookings Papers on Economic Activity, Brookings Institutions, Washington, DC, 1992.

[3]Plexus Group, Commentary #45, "Decision Timeliness and Duration," November 1995.

- Not reviewing your overall investment program—at least once a decade—and putting your conclusions in writing.

- Not reviewing your estate plan once a decade.

- Believing a broker is your friend. Brokers know they make more money when we *believe* they are attentive, nice, and when we *think* they care about us.

- Not recognizing that *inflation* is the investor's unrelenting adversary.

- Paying high fees in the usually mistaken hope that "you get what you pay for" and that high fees are the touchstone of higher returns. It can be true, but it's not necessarily or even usually true. For most investors, avoiding high fees is easy to do and pays off.

If you feel, as I do, that the investor should not pay for the market's normal average rate of return and that fees are better compared to the manager's "surplus" returns *over and above* the market average rate of return, then the stark reality is that actual fees relative to incremental returns are no bargain at all. For investors as a whole, annual fees—when looked at *this* way—are in excess of 100 percent of incremental returns! So investors should really pay attention to fees.[4]

Look at the mistakes other investors make—and learn through their experiences.

One of the best ways to *improve* our long-term average performance is to reduce our errors. Let's look at the mistakes other investors make—and learn through *their* experiences (so we won't have to repeat them). Instead of asking how to make successful investing easier, let's ask the question the other way around: How can investors *make investing harder?* How can investors *reduce their chances of success* and *increase their risk of failure?* What mistakes could we best avoid? Here are two things *not* to do:

- Exercise poor market timing.

- Change managers frequently—always *looking* for *the* very best manager.

[4]Investors can invest in index matching mutual funds. Their management fees and transaction costs are low. Yes, investors will lag behind the market, but *not by much.* They'll do far better than most other investors.

The long, sad history of market timing is clear: Virtually nobody gets it right even half the time. And the cost of getting it *wrong* wipes out the occasional gain of getting it right. So the average investor's experience with market timing is costly. Remember, every time you decide to get out of the market (*or* get in), the investors you buy from and sell to are the best of the big professionals. (Of course, they're not always right, but how confident are you that you will be "*more* right" more often than they will be?) What's more, you will incur trading costs or mutual fund sales charges with each move—and, unless you are managing a tax-sheltered retirement account, you will have to pay taxes every time you take a profit.

America's favorite investor, the remarkably capable, rational, and very successful Warren Buffett, made this important observation in his 1996 annual report to the shareholders of Berkshire Hathaway: "Let me add a few thoughts about your own investments. Most investors, both institutional and individual, will find that the best way to own common stocks is through an index fund that charges minimal fees. Those following this path are sure to beat the net results (after fees and expenses) delivered by the great majority of investment professionals."

Changing managers without good cause is a lot like market timing. The experience of most investors who do this is poor. When should an investment manager be terminated or *fired?*

First, *never* terminate a manager solely for below-market performance over a several-year period. You know from personal experience at ticket counters or tellers' windows that it does not pay to switch from one line to another and then to another. Switching investment managers is even less productive. The manager whose recent-*past* record looks best seldom does best in the following period. If he or she had an ideal environment in the recent past, the near future will likely be inhospitable. Wise investors will choose managers very carefully and then stay the course. Very wise and very well-informed investors will go one step further: Having selected a small group of long-term "finalists," they will pick the manager whose recent results were depressed by an adverse market environment—and get a little extra lift from a subsequently favorable market environment by riding the regression to the mean.

14

THE INDIVIDUAL INVESTOR

INDIVIDUAL INVESTORS ARE DIFFERENT, very profoundly different from institutional investors. And it's not just that individual investors have less money. One difference is decisive: each individual is mortal. Life *is* short and its duration unknown. Inevitable mortality is the dominant reality for all individual investors—as individuals and as investors.

Other important differences between individuals and institutions are also compelling. Those of us who are earning incomes usually have a finite period of years in which to build our lifetime savings and investments. And those who are no longer earning and saving have finite financial resources upon which they will depend for the indefinite duration of their lives.

Another way in which individual investors are different is that their money often takes on great symbolic meaning and can engage their emotions powerfully. Some investors feel their money represents themselves and the worth of their lives (as entrepreneurs often identify their value and their worth with their companies).

Yet another important difference is that individual investors have considerable power to impact others—both financially and emotionally—with gifts and bequests made or not made, or made larger or smaller than anticipated or considered "fair." The emotional power and symbolism of money is often more important than its economic power, and individual investors will be wise to deal carefully with both.

All investors share one formidable and all too easily underestimated adversary: inflation. This adversary is particularly dangerous for individual investors.

For individual investors, inflation is *the* major problem—not the attention-getting daily or cyclical changes in securities prices that most investors fret about. The corrosive power of inflation is truly daunting: At 5 percent inflation, the purchasing power of your money is cut in half in less than 15 years—and cut in half again in the *next* 15 years. At 7 percent, your purchasing power drops to 25 percent of its present level in just 21 years— the elapsed time between "early" retirement at 61 and age 82, an increasingly normal life expectancy. This is clearly serious business, particularly when the individual is retired and has no way to add capital to offset the dreadful erosion of purchasing power caused by inflation.

For individual investors, inflation is the major problem.

Here is a table that shows how increasing inflation cuts into purchasing power.

Rate of Inflation	Time to Cut Your Money in Half
2%	36
3%	24
4%	18
5%	14
6%	12
7%	11

Individual investors are also differentiated from institutional investors by the fact that each of us has responsibilities we take very personally: educating our children, providing security for ourselves and for our loved ones, helping pay the costs of health care for elderly relatives, contributing to the schools and other institutions from which we have benefited or hope our communities will benefit, and so forth. In addition, as individual investors, each of us will want to provide a strong self-defense against catastrophe—including the risk of living longer and needing more health care than anticipated. Finally, most individuals wish to leave something to their children or grandchildren to help enhance their lives. (Our children having better lives is, for most of us, the main meaning of "progress.") Not only are these responsibilities taken very personally, in many cases, the amounts that will be involved are unknown—and may become almost "unlimited." The potential cost of health care in old age is one uncomfortable example.

Most individual investors have a long-term implicit "balance sheet" of assets and responsibilities. However, most investors have not examined their own total financial picture or put it all down on paper. And most have not been explicit about the direct and indirect stakeholders—the "we"—in their balance sheet responsibilities.

In planning the "responsibility" side of your Investor's Balance Sheet, you will want to decide who is included in your "we"—and for what purpose. How much responsibility do you plan to take for your children's education? College is costly. Graduate school is increasingly accepted as the norm, and it's costly too. After providing for education, is help with a child's first home important to you? Help in starting a business or a dental practice? How about your parents, brothers, and sisters, or your in-laws? Under what circumstances would they need your financial help? How much might be involved and when? Be sure you know what your total commitments would add up to and when the money would be needed.[1]

Saving naturally and necessarily comes before investing because we can only invest what we have previously saved. Buying straw hats in the fall or Christmas cards in January and saving through the many other daily forms of conscientious underspending can make a splendid difference over the years—particularly when matched with a sensible long-term approach to investing.

The first purpose of saving is to accumulate a defensive reserve that can be turned to for help—like a fire extinguisher—if and when trouble comes. And like a fire extinguisher, such a reserve should be clearly used

---

[1]The then-president of Consolidated Cigar was thrilled to see his company transformed into a "growth" stock in the early 1960s by the Surgeon General's first reports on smoking and health. Accepting his newfound position as a man of wealth, he pledged $10 million to his alma mater—only to find that as the share price declined back to "normal," he could not fulfill his pledge. But the university had spent the money on a building and sued for payment. A lot of unnecessary emotional harm was done.

boldly and fully whenever needed. If you use your defensive reserve cautiously or only partially, you will simply require a proportionately larger reserve—and it's costly (in opportunity costs) to have a larger reserve than is really needed. So the reserve is on hand to be *spent,* not to be held back in time of need. After providing for protection against serious contingencies, further savings can be invested for the long term.

With enough time, the consequences of the accumulating power of compound interest can be astounding. Consider: $1 invested in common stocks—and held there—from 1926 to 1990 would have compounded (assuming no taxes, commissions, or management fees) into $500 and by 1997, well over $1000! This is nearly incredible—but not wrong. It may seem more plausible after making certain "adjustments." For example, if the annual cost of brokerage commissions and management fees were ½ percent, the final amount would be $350. And if a 28 percent tax were assumed on all income and capital gains, the end amount would be $110. And if adjusted further for inflation (compared with a normally "safe" investment in Treasury bills, which would barely return the original $1 in purchasing power), the end sum from investments in stocks would be $16—sixteen *times* your money—in real purchasing power!

One of the core concepts and basic themes of this book is that funds available for long-term investment will do best for the investor if invested in stocks—and *kept* in stocks through time. But what about elderly investors whose life expectancy is less than the 10 years that approximates "long term"? Shouldn't they, the conventional wisdom would have it, invest primarily in bonds to "preserve capital"? As usual, the conventional wisdom may have got it wrong.

While retired investors may decide for "peace of mind" that they prefer to invest in relatively stable securities with relatively high income, they should know they are letting their emotional interests dominate their economic interests. They may well be right to do so, but not necessarily. For individuals, as for institutions, investing in bonds to generate more current income dooms the individual to Ellis's Law: $1 of extra income costs $1.50 in the total return forgone by not investing as much in long-term equity investments. This may be a heavy price to pay for the apparent conservatism of shifting assets into higher-yielding "defensive" investments such as bonds and income stocks—*and* becoming a stationary target for inflation to do its eroding harm.

Moreover, while the elderly invest*or* may not expect to live for long, the invest*ments*—after being inherited by beneficiaries—may have a very long-term mission. There may be no reason to limit the time horizon of the investments to the owner's lifetime when the owner's true objectives—providing for children, spouse, or alma mater—have a much longer-term horizon.[2]

To be a truly successful lifetime investor, the first and central challenge is to "know thyself"—understand your personal financial goals and what would truly be successful for *you*. As 'Adam Smith' (Jerry Goodman) so wisely counseled: "If you don't know who you are, the stock market is an expensive place to find out!" (So are real estate, commodities, and options.)

Investors will be wise to take time to learn as much as possible about themselves—and how they will feel and behave as investors. For example, here's a simple test—with a friendly twist—that, for most investors, provides some useful insight.

> **Question:** If you had your own choice, which would you prefer?
>
> Choice A: Stocks go *up* by quite a lot—and *stay up* for many years.
>
> Choice B: Stocks go *down* by quite a lot—and *stay down* for many
>   years.

Without looking ahead, which did you choose? If you selected Choice A, you would be joining 90 percent of the professional investors who've taken this little test. Comforting to know most pros are with you? Shouldn't be. Here's why. Unless you are a long-term *seller* of stocks, you would have chosen *against* your own interests if you chose A.

First, remember that when you buy a common stock, what you really buy is the right to receive the dividends paid on that share of stock.[3] Just as we buy cows for their milk and hens for their eggs, we buy stocks for their current and future dividends. If you ran a dairy, wouldn't you prefer to have cow prices low when you were buying, so you could get more gallons of milk for your investment in cows?

The lower the price of the shares when you buy, the more shares you will get for every $1,000 you invest and the greater the amount of dollars you would receive in dividends on your investment. So if you are a saver and a

---

[2]Besides, one of the secrets to a long and happy life is to "keep climbing" and stay, in Disraeli's felicitous phrase, "in league with the future." It keeps us young to invest in stocks.

[3]Yes, you also get the right to vote on the selection of auditors, the election of directors, and so forth. And you get the right to be bought out at a higher price if and when there's a future takeover. But realistically, very few votes of shareholders go against management's recommendation, and unanticipated buyouts occur at very, very few companies—so these shareholder rights are usually not very important compared with dividends. Yes, you also get the right to sell the stock to another investor, hopefully, of course, at a higher price. But what determines the price that next investor will gladly pay? The present value of expected future dividends.

buyer of shares—as most investors are and will continue to be for many years—your real long-term interest is, curiously, to have stock prices go *down* quite a lot and stay there, so you can accumulate more shares at lower prices and thereby receive more dividends with the savings you invest.

So the right long-term choice is the counterintuitive Choice B—it's best for you to have stock prices go way *down* and stay down—so you can acquire more rights to receive more dividends in future years with the money you invest now.

This has been much more than a clever explanation of a question with a twist. It can be the key insight that will enable you to enjoy greater success as an investor *and* greater peace of mind during your investing career.

Most investors, being all too human, much prefer stock markets that *have been* rising and feel most enthusiastic about buying more shares when stock prices are already high—causing the future rate of return from their dividends to be axiomatically low. (The dollars of dividends to be received will be the same per share of stock whether you pay a lot or a little for the shares.) Similarly, most investors feel quite negatively about stocks *after* share prices have gone down and are most tempted to sell out at the wrong time—when prices are already low—and the future dividend yield on the price paid would be high.

If you can use the insight illuminated by our simple quiz and incorporate the *rational* answer into your own investment thinking and *behavior,*

FIGURE 14-1   This chart shows how important reinvesting dividends has been—even in two long periods when stocks achieved virtually no appreciation: the 25 years from 1930 to 1955 and the 20 years from 1965 to 1985. As shown in the chart, $1.00 grew to $48.28 due to price appreciation—but with dividends reinvested that same $1.00 grew to become $1,113.92.

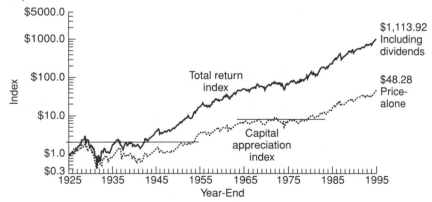

you will appreciate that your human emotions often move contrary to your rational economic interests. You will school yourself to go against the crowd *and* your own feelings—and will strive to avoid the temptation to jump on the bandwagon to buy when stocks are high or to jump off when stocks are low.

Avoid the temptation to buy when stocks are high and sell when stocks are low.

Another all-too-human characteristic of most investors is paying too close attention to the day-to-day—even hour-to-hour—ups and downs of stock prices. Rationally, we know most of the changes in share prices are "noise" or almost random fluctuations. Consider the data: Most stocks will change by 4 percent or more between the high and low prices during each trading day. There are nearly 250 trading days a year, which would imply a total change in prices over the year of 1,000 percent (4 percent × 250 days). But the price of most stocks changes less than 15 percent net over a year, so more than 98 percent of the gross change is just flutter or noise. Investors should ignore the dance of stock prices, fascinating—and seductive—as the activity may be.

If you find yourself getting caught up in the excitement of a rising market or distressed by a falling market, stop. Break it off. Go for a walk and cool down. Otherwise, you will soon become part of the "crowd," wanting to *do* something—and you will start making errors, perhaps grave errors that you will regret.

Individuals with large fortunes—$25 million and over—can obtain good investment counsel as a "separate account." Those with less than $2 million usually cannot. Their accounts are simply too small to be important to a first-rate firm.

Fortunately, all investors do have an alternative: mutual funds. Two types of funds have particular interest. One type is an index fund, run at low costs and fees and designed to replicate any one of several recognized market indexes such as the Standard & Poor's 500 or the Russell 2000[4] (see Chapter 3, The Powerful Plodder).

Closed-end mutual funds are another type that is interesting, specifically those now selling at a discount *and* obliged by their bylaws to become open-end funds—which would eliminate the discount—within a reason-

---

[4]Vanguard offers a series of such funds.

able time period, say five years. Such funds are particularly interesting if their long-term style of investing ("growth" or "value") is currently out of favor and you can buy into them during their "off season."

As with institutional investing, individuals who have a separate account will be wise to agree *in writing* with the investment manager on the overall program by which their funds will be invested: long-term objectives, investment policy constraints, and performance expectations in various market environments. Individuals who invest in mutual funds can do nearly as much by reading carefully the written statement in each fund's prospectus of its long-term objectives, policies, and performance expectations.

You will increase your chances of achieving superior investment performance—which means reliably achieving your own explicit and realistic investment objectives—by taking time once a year for a formal, objective review of your investment objectives, financial resources, financial responsibilities, and recent investment results compared with prior realistic expectations.

While the focus of attention will typically be on investments, the following should also be examined: savings, insurance, bank credit available, current debts, probable obligations to help or support others in your "we" group, annual income versus expenditure, and estate plans. The objective of this disciplined exercise is to "turn on the lights" and look over the whole situation.

If you have successfully saved and invested enough to have ample funds for all chosen responsibilities or obligations, you have truly won the "money game." This is an appropriately thrilling achievement. Winners should be careful never to put their victory back at risk, particularly by unnecessary or injudicious borrowing or by committing too much to any one investment or by overextending responsibilities and commitments. Winners should avoid speculations striving to win *big*. It's not worth the risk of losing enough to become a "non-winner"—not just a loser, but truly a sucker. Winners should also be careful about being "too careful" as noted above: a shift to nominally "conservative" investing can leave investments exposed and at risk to the erosion of inflation. Nathan Mayer Rothschild, the founder of that great family's very great fortune, explained what it takes: "It requires a great deal of boldness and a great deal of caution to make a great fortune; and when you have got it, it requires ten times as much wit to keep it."

As an individual investor, these ten "commandments" may be useful guides to thinking about your decisions on investments:

1. Don't speculate. If you must "play the market" to satisfy some emotional "itch," recognize you are gambling on your ability to beat the pros—

and limit the amounts you play with to those you would gamble with the pros at Las Vegas. (Keep accurate records of your results, and you'll soon convince yourself to quit!) And beware of switching managers to move your money in hot pursuit of the "best" manager. (As in so many domains, striving for *perfection* is the enemy of achieving the *good*.)

2. Don't buy on tips. Ever. No matter how sure you feel a tip *must* be, let it pass. The only good tips depend upon having really important inside information. And using inside information is illegal.

3. Don't do anything in investing primarily for "tax reasons." Tax shelters are poor investments. Tax loss selling is primarily a way for brokers to increase commissions. Two exceptions: making charitable gifts with low-cost stock can make sense *if* you were going to sell the stock anyway. Set up an IRA if you can and maximize contributions to your 401(k) or profit-sharing plan every year.

"It requires a great deal of boldness and a great deal of caution to make a great fortune."

—Nathan Mayer Rothschild

4. Don't think of your home as an investment. Think of it as a place to live with your family, period. Except when inflation surges—as it did in America in the late 1970s—and lifts the replacement cost of real estate *and* drives stock and bond prices down, owning residential real estate is not a great investment. Over the past 20 years, home prices have risen less than the consumer price index and have returned less than Treasury bills.

5. Never do commodities. Consider the experience of a commodities broker who, over a decade, advised nearly *1,000* customers on commodities. How many made money? Not even one.[5] But *he* did, thanks to commissions.

6. Don't be confused about stockbrokers. They are usually very nice people, but their job is not to make money *for* you. Their job is to make money *from* you. While some stockbrokers are wonderfully conscientious

---

[5]*The Money Masters* by John Train (New York: Harper & Row, 1987).

people who are devoted to doing a good, thoughtful job for customers they work with over many, many years, you can't *assume* your stockbroker is working that way for you. Some do, but most simply can't afford it. (The typical stockbroker "talks to" 200 customers with *total* invested assets of $5 million. To earn $100,000 a year, he needs to generate $300,000 in gross commissions, or 6 percent of the money he talks to. To generate this volume of commissions, the broker cannot afford the time to learn what is "right." He has to keep the money moving—and it would be *your* money.)

7. Don't invest in new or "interesting" investments. They are all too often designed to be *sold to* investors, not to be *owned by* investors.[6] And don't believe what you hear from other investors. Most of their stories belong in the proverbial box so carefully labeled by the thrifty Bostonian: "String too short to save."

8. Don't invest in bonds because you've heard bonds are conservative or for safety of either income or capital. Bond prices fluctuate nearly as much as stock prices, and bonds are poor defenses against the real risk of long-term investing: inflation.

9. While respecting money as a store of value and for the good it can do, don't ever let money dominate you. If you find yourself adding it up more than ten times a year, you are probably paying too much attention and are risking getting caught up in the crowd. Figuratively at least, go take a walk and cool off.

10. Don't trust your emotions. When you feel euphoric, you're probably in for a bruising. Don't confuse brains with a bull market. When you feel down, remember it's darkest just before dawn—and take no action. (Remember the test presented in this chapter?) The secret to long-term investment success is benign neglect. Don't try too hard. Activity in investing is almost always in surplus. Leave compounding alone to do its good work for you.

Finally, here are ten friendly suggestions that may prove helpful:

1. Get a pro. Investing is no place for amateurs (any more than the NFL). Be sure you have sensible professionals managing your investments. Books that say "you can do it" are popular—and some sell very well. That's

---

[6]My Aunt Saizie is in her 80s. After years and years of careful saving and wise investing, she built up a portfolio of common stocks worth nearly $100,000. She asked me whether she should take the strong recommendation of a very nice-looking young man from the local broker's office. His proposition: sell all her stocks (incurring a large capital gain) and put most of the money in Treasury bills for safety of principal and then use the rest to buy stock options so she could participate in any bull market that might come along. Fortunately, Saizie is too wise and experienced an investor to get drawn in by something that "interesting." (Imagine the commissions that would have been generated for that broker!)

why they're written. Read and enjoy them as entertainment. But don't believe them.

Andrew Tobias's *The Only Investment Book You'll Ever Need* is different. Particularly worth reading as a primer, it's full of sensible advice and useful information.[7]

2. Write out your long-term goals, your long-term investing program, *and* your estate plan—and stay with them. Review these plans at least once each decade. As every great coach advises his or her athletes: "Plan your play—and play the plan!" Don't procrastinate.

3. If your long-term investment policy is not working out in the short run (e.g., stocks dropped sharply in price), your first assumption should be that you will "double up"—because you *know* you took considerable time and care in making your original policy decision.

Examine your long-term goals and your basic reasoning and the *long-term* evidence you used to be sure they were sound. Be very careful of "current" data from the last few years: such data tend to lead us astray. If the long-term evidence *is* still valid and your reasoning *was* sound, stay the course.

4. Be a student of investing and investors. Concentrate your studies on human psychology (not on the numbers and the financials) because most of the blunders we make are emotional, not computational errors. How your investments behave is beyond your control. But how *you* behave in response to their fluctuation is within your control—and far more important in determining your long-term success.

5. Save.

6. Remember that money holds *powerful*—but different—symbolic meaning for everyone. Respect the meaning others bring to it and the meanings you bring to it. And be careful.

7. If you find yourself tempted to ask a Wall Street "insider" "What stock should I buy?" resist the temptation. If you *do* ask, don't listen to the answer. And if you do *hear* an answer, promise you won't act on it.

8. If you find yourself tempted to feel you are "just an individual investor" and therefore somehow not important, remember it's *your* money. You *are* the client. And your work is the most important part of achieving long-term success with investments.

9. Read the annual reports of Berkshire Hathaway, written by Warren Buffett. He's the most effective investor in securities in America and gives

[7]If you would like to study the history of investment thinking, you might enjoy *The Investor's Anthology,* compiled by Jim Vertin and Charles D. Ellis, published in 1997 by John Wiley & Sons.

extraordinarily valuable lessons in these reports. (On request, they'll send you reprints of past reports; or you can get them via the Internet at www.berkshirehathaway.com.)

10. Remember that while price fluctuations command our attention, the real problem for investors is *inflation.* Price fluctuations come and go. Inflation *persists* and is unrelenting in the damage it does.

Finally, if you have a 401(k) plan where you work, you have a real and direct interest in knowing how your company's 401(k) stacks up in comparison to others. Ask these three key questions:

- Does your plan allow you to contribute the maximum the law permits?

- Does your employer match *all* or part of your own contribution? (Some match dollar for dollar.)

- Does your plan have sufficient investment options so you can construct the long-term investment program that's realistic and really right for you?

If you do have a 401(k) plan, please remember that the freedom to determine the investing program that is best for you is a grave responsibility. Some 401(k) investors will take the time and care to truly understand the market, inflation, and investments, and they will discipline themselves to achieve good results. Others will be fortunate or lucky; things will work out for them much better than could be expected. But others will not be so lucky. They will remind us that "there are old pilots and bold pilots, but no old bold pilots." They'll make mistakes, small and large, and create serious long-term difficulties for themselves and their families.

Be different. Either develop your own long-term program *or* get good advice on sound long-term investment policy—and stick with it.

The exciting independence *and* the serious danger remind me of flying a small airplane. Before you solo, try answering these two friendly "trick" questions:

- Since you began driving a car, in which decade was gasoline actually cheapest?

- What proportion of the typical American's *lifetime* expenditures on health care is spent in the last six months of life?

The answers tell us something about inflation and old age—two important subjects we all will experience, but we all tend to ignore. Here are the answers to our two trick questions:

1.   This decade.

2.   80 percent.

If you are—as I was—skeptical about and surprised by these answers, please take the time to check them both out. Inflation-adjusted, the price of gasoline when you turned 16 really was higher than the price now. Most people underestimate both the compounding impact of inflation and the onerous cost of end-of-life health care. Consider both questions carefully for the logic and insight they can provide to your own way of thinking.

15

CHAPTER

PLANNING
YOUR PLAY

YES, DEATH *IS* EVERY INDIVIDUAL'S ultimate reality. But as an *investor,* you just may be making too much of it. If, for example, you plan to leave most of your capital in bequests to your children, the appropriate time horizon for your *family* investment policy—even if you are well into your 70s or 80s—may well be so long term that you'd be correct to ignore such investment conventions as that canard, "Older people should invest in bonds for higher income and greater safety."

This may *sound* okay, but the more efficacious decision for you and your family is probably to invest 100 percent in equities, because your *investing* horizon is far, far longer than your *living* horizon. The conventional wisdom—"to determine the percentage of your assets you should have in stocks, just subtract your age from 100"—is often wrong for two main reasons: (1) It compels you to reduce the proportion of stocks, and increase the proportion of cash and bonds, with each passing year—which you can do only by selling your stocks, thereby generating a costly and unnecessary tax bill for yourself. (2) If the people you love (your family and heirs) or even the organizations you love (your favorite charities) are likely to outlive you—as they almost certainly will—then you should extend your investment horizon to cover not just your own life span but theirs as well. If, for instance, you are 30 years old with a two-year-old son,

111

your investment horizon is not just another 55 years (your own future life expectancy), but well over a century. Likewise, even if you are 75 years old, your investment horizon could be equally long if you have young grand-children or even a favorite charity.

Don't change your investments just because you have come to a differ-ent age—or have retired. If you can afford fine paintings, you wouldn't change the ones you love most simply because you had reached retirement or had celebrated your 70th or 80th birthday. It's the same with investments: Maintain the strategy you have set for yourself if you can afford to do so.

Don't change your investments just because you have come to a different age.

Remember 'Adam Smith's' wise admonition: "The stock doesn't know you own it." This observation applies to *all* investments: stocks, bonds, buildings, and so forth. All have value today and will have a future value irrespective of who owns them. So investing should always be done for *investment* reasons and not for *personal* reasons such as your own chrono-logical age.

Most investors' actual time horizons for investments are quite *long*—20 years, 30 years, and often 50 years or more—because the investments they pass on to others will continue to be active well past the period of their own lives. We investors *are* mortal, but our investments don't know it—and they don't care.

Compounding is powerful. Remember the grateful sultan who offered to reward his wazir very generously for a great deed that had saved the sul-tan's empire? The wazir modestly offered to accept only one grain of wheat on the first square of a checkerboard, only two grains on the next, just four grains on the third, eight grains on the fourth, and so on—and on and on. The wazir indicated that he had no need for a great reward and that the sym-bolism of this compound giving would please his humble, grateful heart. Joyfully, the Sultan seized upon this seemingly simple way to clear his obli-gation. Sadly, he hadn't reckoned on the formidable power of compound-ing. *Any*thing doubled 64 consecutive times will balloon—and balloon again. In the story, the few grains of wheat compounded to a total value that was greater than *all* the wealth in the entire empire! To defend his honor before Allah, the sultan ended up turning over his entire empire to the wazir.

Here's a variation that should be more familiar to most of us today: If you had invested $100 in shares of common stock at the start of the 20th century, what would that investment be worth today? Quick answer: $733,383! Wow, $100 grew to nearly three-quarters of a million dollars! But not so fast! Let's ask some clarifying questions.

Question: How much of the 95 years' gain came in the last 20 years?

Answer: Most of it. In fact, by 1975, the fund had increased to only $75,000. The other $643,000 came in the last two decades as the stock market flourished.

Question: How much of the apparently wonderful gain was really just the "pass-through" of inflation?

Answer: Most of it. The *real* gain over the entire century was just over $40,000—certainly a substantial gain on $100, but just as certainly, only 6 percent of the *nominal* gain of $733,382.

The main message is *not* how wonderfully compounding increases real wealth. The main message is that inflation relentlessly destroys wealth's purchasing power—*almost* as rapidly as economic gains are building wealth. Only the real *net* gain is spendable. So beware of those promotional materials and advertising that are deceiving investors with a Lorelei promise of phenomenal "riches" in the future *without* explaining the grim negative—and simultaneous—impact of inflation.

Inflation is the ruthless, unrelenting destroyer of your capital. To purchase an item costing $100 in 1960 would have cost $500 in 1995. In other words, during just one generation, inflation reduced the value of each dollar by a withering 80 percent—or 4.8 percent *compounded annually.*

Your investments do not know your wishes or intentions—and they really don't care.

The grinding, corrosive power of inflation is very clearly and emphatically the investor's worst enemy. In just 20 years—as shown in Figure 15-1—the purchasing power of $1.00 shrunk to $.35.

It's even more important for rational, long-term investors to know and remember that in the 15 years from the late 1960s to the early 1980s, the unweighted stock market *adjusted for inflation* plunged about 80 percent. As a result, the decade of the 1970s was actually worse for investors than the decade of the 1930s!

FIGURE 15-1   The shrinking value of $1.00

Source: Consumer Price Index, *U.S. Department of Labor.*

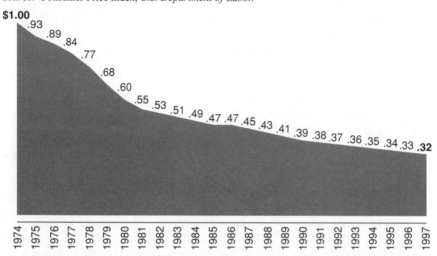

The power of inflation to impose real harm on investments may be seen by studying the Dow Jones Industrial Average *after* adjustment for inflation. Note particularly:

- From 1977 to 1982, the inflation-adjusted Dow Jones Industrials went from 270 to 100—a five-year *loss* of 63 percent!

- In 1993, the Dow Jones was equal to its inflation-adjusted level in 1928. Sixty-five years was a long, long time to wait to get even.

Investors would be wise to study investment history. (Beware the 1950s, when investors finally reset the basic relationships between the returns expected of stocks and the expected returns of bonds, at last shaking off the impact of both the Depression and World War II.) The more you study history, the better—because the more you know about how securities markets *have* behaved in the past, the more you'll understand their true nature and how they *will* behave. Such an understanding enables us to live *rationally* with markets that would otherwise seem irrational. At least we would not get shaken loose from our long-term strategy by the short-term tricks and deceptions of the market's gyrations. (See Figures 15-2 and 15-3.)

In developing a sound financial plan, investors will want to begin with good answers ("good" because they are both *comforting* and *rational*) to these three overarching questions:

- Does my plan assure me of enough income to pay for an appropriate standard of living—*after overcoming inflation*—during retirement?

FIGURE 15-2   Comparison of T-bills, bonds, and stocks over time

Source: Fortune, *December 25, 1995.*

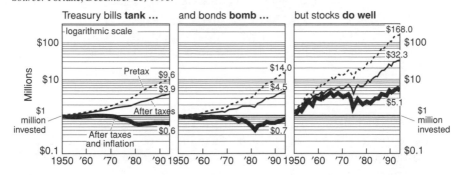

For most people, this "sufficiency of income" works out to 75 to 80 percent of preretirement spending *plus* 3 to 4 percent annually *compounded* to offset inflation.

- Will my financial reserves be sufficient to cover unexpected emergencies—usually health crises—particularly in old age?

    Women live longer than men, and wives are often younger than husbands—so most married men will want to pay particular attention to providing adequately for their wives' years as widows.

- Will the remaining capital match my goals and intentions for giving to my heirs and charities?

If these core questions are not fully and affirmatively answered, your plan needs to be reconsidered and changed—perhaps substantially. Do it now—so you'll have time on your side to work for you as much as possible.

FIGURE 15-3   And the winner is . . .

Source: Wall Street Journal, *May 28, 1996, p. R32.*

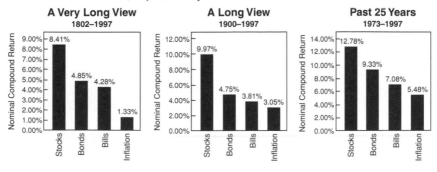

Write down your goals—with the target dates by which you intend to achieve them—so you can measure your actual progress compared to your explicit plan, because in all matters of investing *time* is key.

Investing is not necessarily best when driven by noninvestment events, such as the timing of children's admission to college, receipt of an inheritance, or the date of your retirement. Separate *when* you invest from *how* you invest. Your investments do not know your wishes or intentions—and they really don't care. As an investor, you must adapt to the market. The market won't adapt to you. If today isn't the right time for you to implement a long-term investment program—because the market appears too high— you can always put your capital in safe storage with a money market fund and then convert to long-term investments when you believe market prices are appropriate, or usually more wisely, invest in steady, equal amounts over a several-year period. (This is called *dollar cost averaging,* and it has the happy result that your average purchase price will be less than the average price at which you purchase!)

Over your lifetime as an investor, your optimal investment program will change—and change again—partly because your circumstances and resources will change and partly because your objectives and priorities will change. But the more thoughtfully and soundly you plan, and the further in advance you do so, the less you should need to change your plan as time passes. Planning a sound long-term investment program is often done best in 10-year chunks of time. This is because working with decade-long blocks of time reminds us that sound investing is inherently long term in nature, and our planning will be wiser and more surely thought out when explicitly considered over the long, long term.

Of course, *planning* is only as useful as the actual *implementation* that follows. Investors will want to follow the wise coach's great twin admonitions: "Plan your play. And play your plan."

The first step is clear: *Get out of debt.* It's a well-earned, great feeling when you achieve the first victory of paying off your school loans and the debts incurred when setting up your first household.

The key to getting out of debt is clear: Save! A lifetime based on the habit of thrift—spending less than you might and deferring the spending you do—is essential to saving. Those who assume or hope their incomes will somehow outstrip their spending may believe in magic, but they are doomed to be disappointed, often grievously. "Pay yourself first" by putting money into your savings on a regular basis. A dollar-cost-averaging account at a mutual fund, which will automatically—and safely—deduct a fixed dollar amount each month from your bank account or your paycheck, is a very good way to pay yourself first.

There's a big difference between deliberate *borrowing* and *being in debt*. The *borrower* is comfortable because he or she has ample capacity to repay and, most important, decides or controls the timing of payment. The *debtor* borrows only what a lender decides to lend—and must repay at the behest of the *lender.* (Just as borrowing differs from being in debt, retirement differs from old age. In retirement, you have more time for travel, reading, sports, and other interests. In old age, your body aches in different ways *every* day. And every night.)

Look at Figure 15-4. If you are age 30 (reading in the second column of the table), you'll need to accumulate *$2.5 million* when you reach age 65 to produce $35,000 a year of real spending money. The column shows—for each level of savings you've *already* accumulated—how much you'll have to save *every* year to achieve that goal.

Note the rather favorable assumptions: All your savings go into a tax-free account, such as a 401(k) plan, where they are further assumed to compound at 10 percent annually until retirement at age 65. In the future (starting from present market levels), this will be possible, but not easy—even if you invest entirely in equities. In bonds, it simply cannot be done.

Figure 15-4 tells an important story about *inflation.* The figures in the top row, entitled "Nest-egg goal" are the amounts you would need to have saved by age 65 to have the inflation-adjusted equivalent of $35,000 in yearly spending money. (If you'd want $70,000 a year of spending money to sustain your lifestyle, multiply the top row figures by 2; if you'd want $105,000, multiply by 3, and so forth.) Here's how to read the table:

FIGURE 15-4   What it will take to get there from here

Your current age	25	30	35	40	45	50	55
Nest-egg goal	$3 mil.	$2.5 mil.	$2.1 mil.	$1.7 mil.	$1.4 mil.	$1.1 mil.	$.94 mil.

How Much You Need to Save Annually

Your current savings							
$0	$6,890	$9,248	$12,524	$17,217	$24,300	$36,004	$58,995
$10,000	$5,868	$8,211	$11,463	$16,116	$23,125	$34,689	$57,367
$25,000	$4,334	$6,656	$9,872	$14,463	$21,363	$32,717	$54,926
$50,000	$1,777	$4,064	$7,220	$11,709	$18,427	$29,430	$50,857
$100,000	$0	$0	$1,916	$6,201	$12,554	$22,856	$42,720
$250,000	$0	$0	$0	$0	$0	$3,315	$18,308

- Find your present age in the top row.

- The *nest-egg goal* is the amount of capital you will need to accumulate to have an *inflation-adjusted* $35,000 to spend each year from age 65 on.

- The *current savings* on the left—ranging from $0 to $250,000—is the amount invested tax-free at a return of 10 percent annually until you reach age 65.

- The rest of the table shows how much you would need to save and invest each year to achieve your nest-egg goal.

- After retirement at age 65, the assumed returns average 7 percent. And at age 90, it is further assumed, all your accumulated savings will have been entirely spent.

Remember algebra and solving equations with two unknowns? Did your course get to three unknowns? As investors, we are confronted by the much more complex challenge: to solve, or at least manage sensibly and rationally, a puzzle with *five* major unknowns—each of which is *changing*. The five unknowns are as follows:

- Rates of return on investments

- Inflation

- Spending

- Taxes

- Time

One analysis[1] of 35 years' experience (from 1960 to 1995) starts with the happy assumption that an investor retired in 1960 with a cool $1 million. The consequences of various investment programs are then examined. The *nominal* compound rates of return for this period were apparently quite encouraging: 10.1 percent for stocks, 7.4 percent for bonds, and 6.1 percent for Treasury bills (or cash equivalents). The very pleasing—but as we'll soon see, very *deceptive*—theoretical final portfolio values produced by the initial $1 million after 35 years are as follows:

Stocks	$28.6 million
Bonds	$12.2 million
T-bills	$8.0 million

[1]Sanford C. Bernstein & Co. Inc., published in revised form in *The Journal of Investing,* spring 1996, pp. 5–16.

Everyone's a *winner!* Or so it may *appear.* But here's how the results look *after taxes:*

Stocks	$15.0 million
Bonds	$5.5 million
T-bills	$3.5 million

What a difference those taxes make—particularly to bonds and T-bills. Note that the taxes assumed are minimal: The investor pays only federal taxes (no state or local taxes!), has no other sources of taxable income, and files a joint return. For most investors able to invest $1 million, actual taxes are almost certain to be larger.[2]

Now, brace yourself for the impact of *inflation,* because that's the way we convert *nominal* or *apparent* values into *real* money. The results are quite sobering. Here's the result *after adjusting for inflation* over the same 35 years:

Stocks	$2.9 million
Bonds	$1.1 million
T-bills	$0.7 million

Inflation is a far larger problem for investors than *taxes.* In real purchasing power, bonds are only 10 percent ahead of the initial investment—after a whole *generation.*[3] And T-bills are actually *behind* the starting line by 30 percent! That's why taxes and inflation are rightly called fearsome "fiscal pirates."

It would be worse if the study had included realistic ownership *costs* such as mutual fund expenses and trading costs. Even the typical money market mutual fund, a common way to manage cash, charges roughly 0.5 percent per year in expenses, while bond funds charge 1 percent and stock funds around 1.4 percent. At those rates, you would have the following take-home results:

[2]The effective tax rate on stocks is far lower than the effective tax on bonds, because part of the return on stocks is market appreciation, and the capital gains tax rate is lower and payment is often deferred many years—or until you decide to sell. A reasonable estimate of the actual or effective federal tax rate on returns from stocks is about 20 percent—or about half the tax rate on income from bonds or bills.

[3]Note that in all but one year since 1950, if you invested in municipal bonds and then held and reinvested for 20 years, you lost. In that one favorable initial investment year, you made 0.01 percent annually after inflation—but before custody or management expenses.

Stocks	$1.8 million
Bonds	$755,000
T-bills	$589,000

And to earn the long-term "average" return, you would have been required to have enough persistent fortitude to stay fully invested when the market dropped *and* inflation was tearing away at your portfolio (*and* your confidence *and* determination to stay the course was faltering).

Spending is the next key factor. Again, time makes all the difference. Consider the consequences of two commonly used spending rules. One investor's rule is to limit spending to a moderate rate (such as 5 percent) of your capital. If you followed this spending rule, as does Mr. 5 Percent, and your investments were entirely in bonds, your $1 million would have fallen in *real* money—or purchasing power—to just $200,000. The all-stock portfolio alternative is, of course, better, but not by much. It would be up about 30 percent—less than 1 percent a *year*.

Another spending rule is to limit spending to cash income (that is, the investor spends only the cash income of a stock portfolio) as dividends and interest payments are received. This investor starts out having *less* to spend than does Mr. 5 Percent—but soon catches up and goes ahead in spending *more*. Compounding is at work again.

Let's look behind the deceptive simplicity of the first of these two widely accepted spending rules: "5 percent of capital" may be okay for your alma mater, but colleges pay no taxes and can expect to receive future contributions from alumni and others to help keep up with inflation. If you *know* you won't live long, that *may* be okay for you, too. But if you live a long time and you spend a dollar amount equal to 5 percent of your original capital, your annual income from interest and dividends will be less than the 5 percent you'll be spending each year. So you'll have to invade capital to draw down the full 5 percent each year. The impact on your invested principal will be increasingly negative—at an accelerating rate— as your declining capital base is required to produce a higher and higher proportion in spendable funds to produce the 5 percent that had originally appeared too moderate.

If you are not confident enough to invest entirely in stocks *and* limit spending to dividends—so that your capital is protected and allowed to grow—then you could invest partly in bonds and reinvest enough of the bond interest to preserve the purchasing power of the bonds. However, since inflation can hit bonds hard *and* irregularly, managing this adjustment can be quite difficult for most investors.

A second spending rule is to spend only from your stock dividends—on the assumption that the companies will take the earnings *not* paid out as dividends and reinvest them productively in their own businesses, enabling earnings and dividends to grow enough to outpace inflation. The rate of spending that derives from the dividends-only approach is approximately 3 percent of capital (or only 60 percent of the 5 percent specified in the other rule).

Beware a subtle danger: An investor can almost always produce more income from a portfolio by investing more and more heavily in income stocks. But other investors *are* rational, and they'll let *you* get more today only if *they* can expect more tomorrow. So part of what appears to be high current income is really a return of capital. (For example, so-called high-yield bonds may appear to pay, say, 7 percent interest, but part of that payment is actually a *return of capital*—the capital that's needed to offset occasional, but probable, defaults.)

Money links the past with the present and the present with the future as a medium of stored value. You can estimate the dollars you'll want to spend each year and, at a spending rate such as 3 percent, the wealth required to produce the income to meet that level of spending. Determine what you have now and what you will save each year. Then see whether you can achieve your capital-accumulation objectives through a sensible investing program. If the first plan you design doesn't work out, you go around again: saving more each year *or* working and saving for more years *or* having less to live on. Be careful: Being optimistic will *not* help. Be cautious and conservative with each assumption: your saving rate, your rate of return, and your spending assumptions.

Combining your saving and capital *objectives* with your realistic *rate-of-return* expectations and your available *time horizon,* you can work out your own *investor's triangulation* to see what amount of capital or savings you will need to contribute each year to your long-term investments to be truly successful in achieving your realistic objectives for spendable money during retirement. (Your accountant or your investment adviser can certainly help you with the calculations.)

If you're surprised at how much you'll need to save and invest each year to meet retirement goals, it may be modestly comforting to know you are not alone. Retirement is expensive—partly because we live longer than did our parents or grandparents, but primarily because inflation is such a powerful and unrelenting opponent.

For investors who do (or will) depend on their annual income from investments, the good news is that, while interest paid on T-bills or on bonds has fluctuated and will fluctuate (sometimes substantially) from year to year, dividends on a portfolio of common stocks will virtually never go down and will generally rise at approximately the rate of inflation.

Time is key in many ways. How long will you be saving? How long and how much will you be spending? How will the arrival of children, or a new career, or future illness, change your spending and saving needs? How will investment opportunities differ over the years during which you invest? The careful study of investing history can be very useful to investors—but which history or which period of history should we study? After a wonderfully long and favorable market in America, there is a natural temptation to think the past 15 years are representative of history. They're not—any more than the beautiful days of summer define the climate of New England.

Investors may ponder the double-edged irony of death. If death comes sooner than expected and planned for, the resources saved over many years may go, at least partially, unused by the saver. If death comes much *later* than planned for, the saved-up resources may be too small, and a grim poverty can result. Be prudent, but don't be prudent to excess. You *can* save too much—and those who love you do not want you to suffer a life of self-enforced poverty just so they can have extra money to spend after you're gone.

The very best bargain for a long-term investor is to obtain sound investment counseling that leads to a sensible long-term investing program most appropriate to that particular investor. Ironically, most investors do not seek—and are unwilling to pay for—real help on developing an optimal long-term investment program. This grievous sin of omission incurs great *opportunity cost*—the cost of missing out on what might so easily have been.

Ironically, most investors will typically pay substantially more for such "implementing details" as investment management fees, stockbrokerage commissions, and custody expenses than they would even *consider* paying for overall investment counseling on their optimal long-term investment program. To be specific, most investors could obtain very good investment counseling for a fee of less than $10,000 (paid only once each decade) and a sound estate plan for less than $20,000 (with 10-year modifications for less than $5,000).

However, most investors would be unwilling to pay this much. Yet the same individuals *will* regularly pay more than $10,000 per million dollars *every year* in such investment operating expenses as brokerage commissions, advisory fees, and custody expenses. It's ironic that investors will—however innocently—pay more for the lesser value.

Pick one day a year (for example, your birthday, New Year's Day or Thanksgiving) as *your* "day away for investing" and pledge to spend a quiet hour or so on that day every year quietly and systematically answering the following questions *in writing.* (After the first annual review, which may take several hours, you'll be updating the plan you wrote out *last* year, so it won't take more than a few hours. You can make those few hours even more productive by rereading last year's plan a week or so *before* your "day away" so it will be fresh in your mind and in your subconscious—where so much good thinking and rethinking can be done.) These questions will help to define and articulate your objectives:

- During retirement, how much income do I want to have each year—in addition to Social Security and my employer's pension benefit?

- How many years will I be in retirement? (The key here is to estimate how long you'll live. Ask your doctor how to apply the average life span of your parents or grandparents to get a reasonable fix on your own "genetic envelope"—appropriately adjusted for the healthfulness of your personal lifestyle.)

- What spending rule am I ready to live with and live by?

- How much capital will I need to provide amply for retirement?

- After insurance, what capital will I need—inflation adjusted—to cover full health care for my spouse and myself? (Your family doctor or your local hospital can give you reasonable estimates based on their experience with people whose medical histories are similar to yours.)

- How much capital do I want to pass on to each member of my family and to any special friends?

- How much capital do I wish to direct to my philanthropic priorities?

Next comes an easy-to-use solution to what most investors consider the truly difficult part of the problem: estimating long-term average annual rates of return on your investments. Here's how:

- First, recognize that over the long, long term, *after adjusting for inflation,* average returns for each type of investment are approximately as follows[4]:

Stocks	4½ percent
Bonds	1½ percent
T-bills	1¼ percent

[4]Precise figures for the 30 years from 1965 to 1994 are *before* adjusting for the 5.4 percent inflation actually experienced: 6.7 percent for cash reserves, 7.0 percent for bonds, and 9.9 percent for stocks. (Courtesy of Ibbotson Associates.)

Thus, if you are operating on the assumption that you can see *real* returns of 10 percent a year from stocks, you are wrong.

- Second, comfortably in advance of your "annual day alone," ask representatives of three organizations this question in writing: "Over the past 20 years, the stock market's average annual total return has been *X* percent. Starting at the stock market's present price level, what average annual rate of return from today's market level would your firm expect over the *next* 20 years?" Next question: "Over the next 1-, 5-, and 20-year periods, what rate of inflation do you expect?" When you have their answers, take the *average* of their answers. (No, it won't be precise, but it will be roughly accurate—and *useful*.) You'll now have two crucial estimates of the future: the nominal rate of return for the stock market and the amount you will have to adjust nominal returns to estimate the real (inflation-adjusted) rates of return.

- Third, remember and act upon the understanding that over the truly long term, the most important investment decisions seem almost obvious. Here are the two most important decision rules:

  —Any funds that will stay invested for 10 years or longer should be in stocks.

  —Any funds that will be invested for *less* than two to three years should be in "cash" or money market instruments.

Your next step is to prepare a complete inventory of your investment *assets,* including the following:

- Investments in stocks and bonds

- Equity in your home

- Assets in any retirement plans, including IRAs, Keoghs, and 401(k) or 403(b) plans

Over the long term, benign neglect really does pay off.

Next, review your retirement income. (You can get help from your employer's human resources department or from your own accountant.) Here are the obvious sources:

- Pension benefits
- Social Security
- Income from your investments

Next come your desired bequests to family (and others) and your intended charitable contributions.

In investing over the longer run, benign neglect really does pay off. After basic decisions on long-term investment policy have been made with care and rigor, you should—with great respect—hold onto them. The problem, as Shakespeare put it, "lies not in our stars, but in ourselves," so, above all else, resist the insidious temptation to *do something*. "Nervous money never wins," say poker players. And they know. At Vail, the Kinderheim's experience-based sign reads:

- LEAVE YOUR KIDS
  FOR THE DAY . . . $5
- YOU WATCH . . . $10
- YOU HELP . . . $25

Before making any commitments that are large in proportion to total wealth, the investor would be wise to reread *King Lear.*

16

ENDGAME

INVESTORS CAN—AND CERTAINLY SHOULD—substantially increase their lifetime success by giving appropriate attention to what chess players know is important: the *endgame.*

Deciding what will be done with your capital to maximize its real useful value can be just as important as deciding how to save, accumulate, and invest it. Providing for your retirement is one of three important challenges. Bequests and gifts to those you love is another. The third—"giving back" to our society—can be exciting and fulfilling.

Wealth *is* power—both the power to do good and the power to do harm. Greater wealth means greater power. Investors who have enjoyed substantial success should give careful consideration—no matter what their hopes or intentions—to whether the amount of wealth they could transfer to their children might do real harm by distorting their offspring's values and priorities or by taking away their descendants' joy of making their own way in life. It's well to recall Lord Acton's words, "Power tends to corrupt and absolute power corrupts absolutely." As we know, too often poor little rich kids *are* miserable. While Mae West was speaking for herself when she announced that "too much of a good thing is *wonderful,*" a large inheritance is not necessarily wonderful for your children. That's why Warren Buffet and Bill Gates have both announced they'll give most of their money away.

Since money is such an effective way to store or transfer value, the investor with a surplus beyond his or her own lifetime's wants and needs will have the opportunity to make a difference to others. Blessed is the investor whose assets do *good;* cursed are those who, despite all their best intentions, cause *harm.*

A large inheritance is not necessarily wonderful for your children.

Before outlining some of the possibilities for transfers within the circle of those you love or feel responsibility for, let's remember that money has powerful symbolic meaning. Psychiatrists marvel that while patients talk rather extensively and relatively early in therapy about relationships with parents, childhood experiences, central hopes and fears, and even such normally very private matters as dreams and sexual experiences, the one subject almost never discussed is . . . *money.*

Most people find it very difficult to discuss money matters openly, fully, rationally, and wisely. So it's best to be especially thoughtful and cautious when making plans about how your money will pass to others. Yes, it's your money now and while you live—but neither of these cheerful current realities is forever. And money is the thermonuclear device among symbols: It symbolizes a *lot*—in different ways for different people, often in quite unexpected ways.

You'll want to get expert legal advice when formulating a sound estate plan, but here are some items for consideration—recognizing that each person will have his or her own objectives and resources and will want to make his or her own decisions:

1. Everyone who can qualify for an Individual Retirement Account (IRA) should have one. And everyone who can possibly afford to do so should contribute the (now $2,000) maximum every year, enabling the twin engines of long-term compounding and tax-free status to do their magic.

Get your children or grandchildren started early. You can give an IRA contribution of up to $2,000 per year to each child or grandchild—starting from the moment they arrive in the delivery room.

2. You can give up to $10,000—without tax—to *each* person you wish *every* year. Married couples can give $20,000 annually to each person. For most investors, these annual gifts can, over time, be a central, even dominant part of a lifelong estate planning and investment managing program.

(Gifts to young children can be made in care of a parent as custodian under the Uniform Gift to Minors Act.)

You might concentrate on your children. Such gifts can really mount up (partly because the future investment income earned on the sums given is taxed at the child's tax rate, which is almost certain to be far less than yours). Over 20 years, $10,000 given annually can, with sensible investing, accumulate to the better part of $500,000.

The main advantage of these gifts is in completely sidestepping the estate tax when you die. Again, the keys to success are *time* and *compounding*—so plan well, start early, and stay with your plan.

3. You have a lifetime limit of $1 million on other tax-free gifts to individuals. A serious look at estate tax tables—particularly at the highest rate you're likely to incur—will strongly encourage you to use this right to give. And contemplation of the cumulative consequences of compound interest will encourage you to use it relatively early in life.

4. Despite the Elizabethan laws against "perpetuities," the IRS allows you to put up to $1 million into a generation-skipping tax-free family fund—to finance education—on which you incur *no* estate tax. (Your children can decide how their trust's assets will be divided among your descendants.) Gift or estate taxes must be paid before the assets pass to this fund. However, once this initial tax is paid, the assets can grow and accumulate in a gift, estate and generation-skipping tax-free environment for several generations within your family, typically for as many as 80 to 100 years. Remember that if investments increase 7 percent per annum after income tax, they will double every 10 years, and $1 million will become $1 billion in 100 years. In the meantime, this family fund can operate as a family bank by allowing distributions or loans to family members as needed. Wealthy investors should consider this option.

A curious provision—called a Qualified Personal Residence Trust—enables you to transfer ownership of your house to your children and live in your own home rent-free for a period of time (such as 15 years). You save substantially on estate taxes—unless you die before the trust matures—while ownership passes to your children.

For example, a $1 million home can be transferred as a taxable gift valued at only 10 to 20 percent of the current market value for this reason: The IRS considers the taxable *present* value of the gift to be *only* the value of the children's right to take possession at the end of the 15-year term of the trust. (The discount to a low present value is the obverse of the powerful accumulation or growth generated by compound interest.)

Money symbolizes a lot—in different ways for different people.

5. If you wish to transfer substantial sums to your descendants, but you worry about distorting their values and lives with too much money at too early an age—before they reach "fiscal maturity"—then consider an arrangement used by Jackie Onassis.[1]

Here's the general idea: A trust can be established for, say, 30 years with interim annual distributions of income payable to your favorite school or charity (either at a set dollar amount or as a percentage of the trust's assets)—with the trust *corpus*[2] paid after the 30-year term to the chosen beneficiaries. There's no estate tax and a gift tax is paid only on the estimated net present value of the trust's corpus after discounting at the IRS's prescribed interest rate—an amount that is only a fraction of the probable market value of the corpus 30 years hence.

If you are concerned about the harm that might be done in a *current* wealth transfer to a 30- to 35-year-old beneficiary, but you are sanguine that the same transfer in the *future* would not harm the values of that same person at age 60 or 65, this sort of trust can be an effective way to transfer substantial wealth with minimal tax. (Noting that the key figures are all based on long-term *estimates* of market valuations far in the future, the wise investor will want to work out the specific term of the trust and the investment policy under several different scenarios and select the choice with which he or she feels most confident and comfortable.)

6. Curiously, and quite accurately, estate lawyers will advise that one of the best assets to use for charitable giving at your death may be your currently *tax-exempt* defined contribution retirement fund—401(k), 403(b), IRA, or profit-sharing plan.

This surprising anomaly is true because these assets must be included in your estate. And this means not only that you incur the estate tax, but that you also incur a capital gains tax on the difference between cost and market on your date of death. However, both of these taxes are avoided if you decide to donate the capital to charity. That's why the anomaly: Although tax-free during your working and retirement years, your defined contribution plan is subject to significant taxes upon your death. So for tax efficiency, you may want to draw upon this part of your total wealth for charitable gifts.

---

[1]But reversed by her children under an optional provision in her will.

[2]The principal, or main body, of the money—from the Latin for "body."

Inverted or upside-down reasoning can be a usefully mind-freeing way to explore any complex issue. Investors can think of estate taxes not as a tax on *wealth,* but as a tax on your *reluctance to make irrevocable decisions* while living (particularly long, long before your death) about the distribution of your wealth.

Most investors are *not* willing to make these wealth-distribution decisions. But please remember, the power of compound interest can be used for the maximum period to have the maximum impact on achieving your carefully considered goals and objectives *only if you are willing to make decisions about the future now.*

If you are willing and able to make irrevocable decisions *now* regarding the long-term future disposition of your capital, you can save substantially on taxes. As Ben Franklin wisely said, "A penny saved is a penny earned."

Maximizing your lifetime financial success has *five* stages, or dimensions:

- Earning

- Saving

- Investing

- Contributing

- Estate planning

Ideally, you will maximize achievement in each area along your own value criteria within the feasible set of opportunities available to you—as you enjoy a full and balanced life.

Investors who have conscientiously worked to *maximize* the amount of their savings and investments will want to give comparable attention to *minimizing* the diversion of funds caused by taxes, particularly estate taxes. This effort will maximize the amount of funds devoted to achieving their desired objectives.

Investors with surplus funds beyond the amount they wish to transfer to members of their families and others they care for should not overlook the profoundly rewarding opportunities they may have created for themselves to cause good things to happen.

"Giving money away to charity" puts the whole proposition the wrong way. Instead, think in terms of imaginatively and vigorously *using* your money—the stored values you and your skills have created over many years—to make good things happen for and through the people and organizations you care about. You can derive a great deal of pleasure and personal spiritual fulfillment in the process of making a positive difference in people's lives.

Think of your money as the stored values
that you and your skills have created.

Select those actions or changes that would give you deep spiritual satisfaction or pleasure to see coming to fruition. You make these good things come true by committing capital to help *make* it happen. Like many others, you may find gratification in converting your financial resources into actions and values you truly care about. After all, your financial resources are really the stored up consequences of your own hard work, imagination, and good fortune. Here are some opportunities to make an impact:

- Establish scholarships for young people of great talent who aspire to make significant contributions in the arts, science, or business.

- Contribute to scholarships for youth who've gotten a bad deal in life and need someone's help to get on the right road. (If you don't have a particular school in mind, consider Berea College, which accepts *only* kids who can't afford a college education.)

- Provide financial support for science or medicine or social justice— through institutions or groups or individuals.

- Support hospitals, shelters, and other institutions to help those in severe need.

- Supply funding for the arts—music or dance or theater—that can so enrich our lives.

Your greatest satisfaction may come from serving a major national institution, a global organization, or a small entity in your own neighborhood. Experienced charitable activists agree that while contributing money *is* important, even greater enjoyment and satisfaction accrues when you also make a substantial commitment of your time, skill, and energy. Don't to leave this important part of your whole life experience in storage in the attic or the bank—or for someone else to enjoy doing. Look around. Get involved through an active, long-term program of strategic giving.

Contributors have learned how greatly they can enjoy seeing the wealth they have created—by adding economic value at work through producing and delivering better services and products—come to life yet *again* by reducing the constraints on individuals or society and enabling good things to happen during their lives and in ways that matter to them. As the old saying has it, "You can't take it with you!" Those who give something back invariably speak of this dimension of their lives with genuine satisfaction. And those who contribute *more* find they enjoy even *greater* satisfaction.

Contributing your time, talent, and money can be profoundly rewarding in two ways. For yourself, there is great personal satisfaction in seeing how real, living people and organizations benefit. And there are very satisfying personal experiences in engaging productively with stimulating and interesting people—and making new and valuable friendships.

One of my personal "lightbulbs" lit up while I was enjoying clams at Charley O's restaurant in Rockefeller Center in 1974. Huge black-and-white photographs of movie stars decorated the walls; each had a one-liner quote under the picture. The movie star looming over my table was the once very dissolute Tasmanian swashbuckler, Errol Flynn. His quote: "Any guy who dies with more than $10 grand has made a mistake." While Flynn surely had other things in his mind, I resolved there and then to avoid the mistake of paying more than necessary in estate taxes—by giving during my lifetime. I prefer to have made some errors of *commission* (giving sometimes to causes that later disappoint) rather than errors of *omission* (giving too little or too late). It's been interesting and fun—and very rewarding.

As with other areas of investing, it's wise to plan ahead, wise to be conservative (within limits), and wise to make productive use of time by beginning early and sustaining your commitments over as long a time as you can provide yourself.[3]

---

[3]Claude Rosenberg, in addition to authoring several good books on how to make money in investing, has written *Wealthy and Wise*—a fine, pioneering book on how to think through what you can afford to contribute.

CONCLUSION

YOU—**NOT YOUR PROFESSIONAL** investment managers—have the most important job in successful investment management. Your central responsibilities are to decide on your long-term investment objectives and, with the expert advice of professional managers, determine a well-reasoned and realistic set of investment policies that can achieve your objectives.

Only by separating responsibility for investment *policy* from responsibility for portfolio *operations* can you delegate to a manager the authority to implement policy in daily portfolio operations without abdicating your responsibility for defining objectives and making sure that investment policies are designed to achieve your chosen objectives.

The great purpose of investment policy is to provide sound guidance, particularly when market conditions are most distressing and create the most urgent anxiety about the true wisdom of those policies.

You should study your total investment situation and your emotional tolerance of risk and the history of investment markets, because a mismatch between the market's sometimes grim realities and your financial and emotional needs can result—and has resulted—in great harm.

Investors who study the realities of investing will be able to protect themselves and their investments from the all-too-common but unrealistic belief that they can find portfolio managers who will substantially "beat the market." These well-informed investors will understand that the only way an active investment manager can beat the market is to find and exploit other investors' mistakes more often than they find and exploit his and that the manager who strives to beat the market is all too likely to try too hard—and be beaten instead.

So many investment managers are so very good at their work that they don't make enough mistakes; therefore, it is unlikely that any large institutional investor will be able to beat his professional competitors, either substantially or consistently. Most of the managers and clients who insist on trying, either on their own or with professional managers, will be disappointed by the results. It *is* a loser's game.

Happily, there is an easy way to win the loser's game by *not playing*—at least not playing by the conventional rules that are now so out of date. As George Marshall counseled his senior officers on the way to winning World War II: "Don't fight the problem." Accept reality. As expert card players advise, "Play your hand as it lays."

Times have changed. Even as the existing old ways of managing portfolios to beat the market have become obsolete, a new approach is now available—and works. It downplays portfolio operations, particularly of the heroic variety, and concentrates on carefully thought through, well-documented, and well-defined *policy*.

Recognizing that higher returns are the incentive and reward for investors taking—and sustaining—an above-average market risk and that the highest returns therefore come from equity investments, you should set your portfolios' asset mix at the highest ratio of equities that your economic and emotional limitations can afford and sustain over the long term.

To do your work well, you must understand the turbulent nature of markets in the short term and the basic consistency of markets in the long term. This understanding will enable the effective client to increase his or her tolerance for interim market fluctuations and to concentrate on the long-term purpose of the portfolio, taking appropriate full advantage of any investor's greatest resource: time.

Losing is an everyday reality: Stock prices go up and down daily. Inflation corrodes the purchasing power value of investments—day after day. The challenge—and the opportunity—is to lose *less*.

After nearly 50 years on Wall Street, an industry statesman[1] was asked by a young aspirant for the secret of lifetime success in investing. His brief and direct answer: "Don't lose!" It seemed almost too clever at first, but as

---

[1]Joseph K. Klingenstein, senior partner and patriarch of Wertheim & Co.

my understanding has matured, I now recognize his comment as profound wisdom. He got it right.

Tommy Armour, the great golf instructor, wisely advised: "Hit the shot that makes the next shot easy!" General George Patton said it this way: "Let the other poor, dumb son-of-a-bitch give up his life for his country." They are all talking about the same thing: Don't be heroic. It doesn't pay.

Soundly conceived, persistently followed long-term investment policy *is* the pathway to success in investing. The actions required are not complicated. The real challenge is to commit to the discipline of long-term investing and to avoid the compelling distractions of the excitement that surrounds, but is superfluous to, the real work of investing. This commitment to the discipline of long-term investing is the principal responsibility—and opportunity to contribute—of the *client*. To win the loser's game of "beat the market" is easy: *don't play it.* Concentrate on the winner's game: defining and adhering faithfully to sound investment policy that's right for the market realities and right for your long-term goals and objectives.

You now know all you will ever need to know to be truly successful with investments—as a successful *client* of professional investment managers.

INDEX